Because Black Is Beautiful

Reflective Imagery & Affirmations for Queens of All Ages

by Charmaine L. Dworkin

Kilanu World Publishing

DEAR BLACK GIRLS

THERE IS NO ONE IN THE WORLD BETTER THAN YOU.

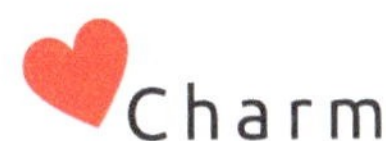

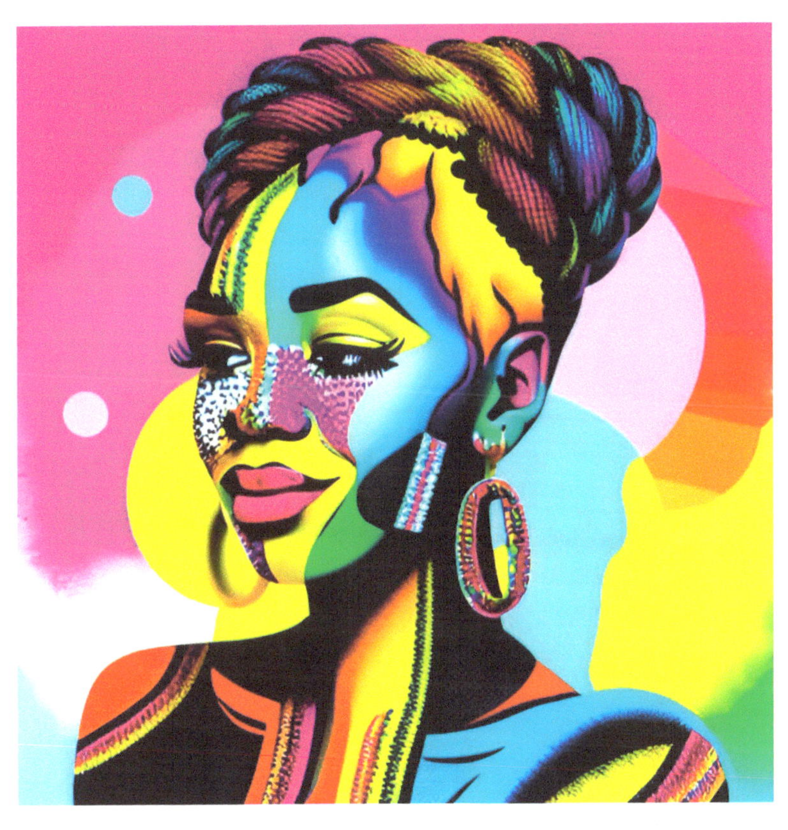

I believe in myself. I can do anything when I apply myself.

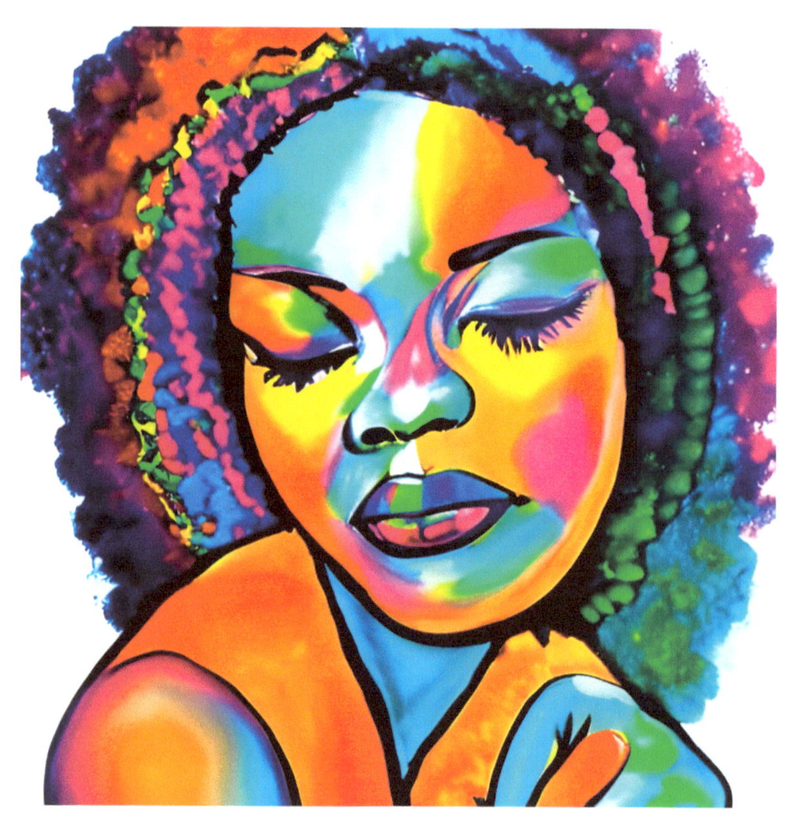

I am soft and tough, both resilient and fragile.

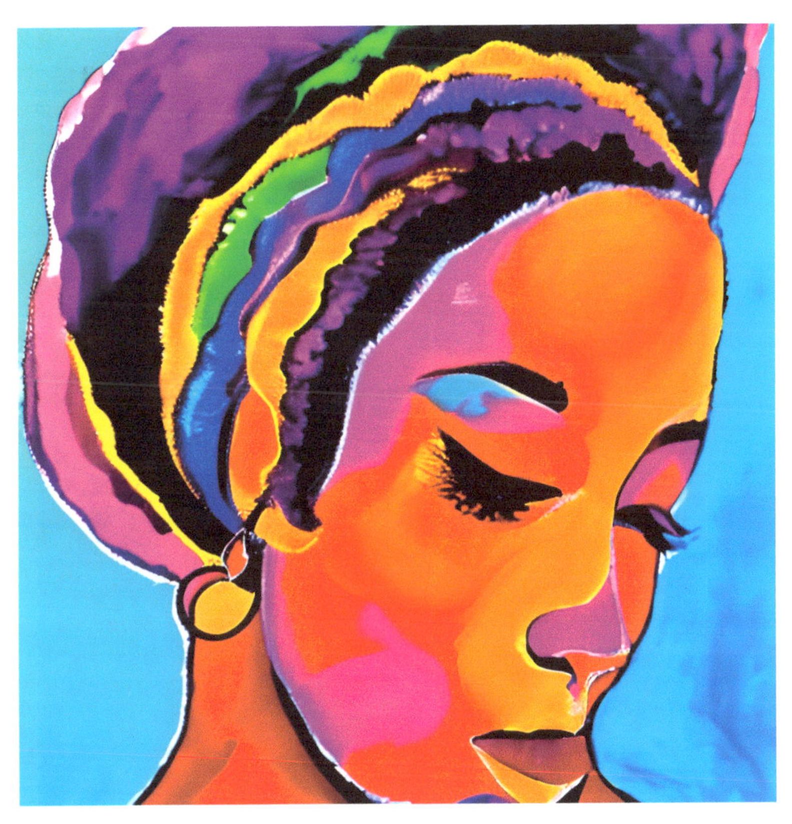

I rise above negativity
and I'll continue to rise.

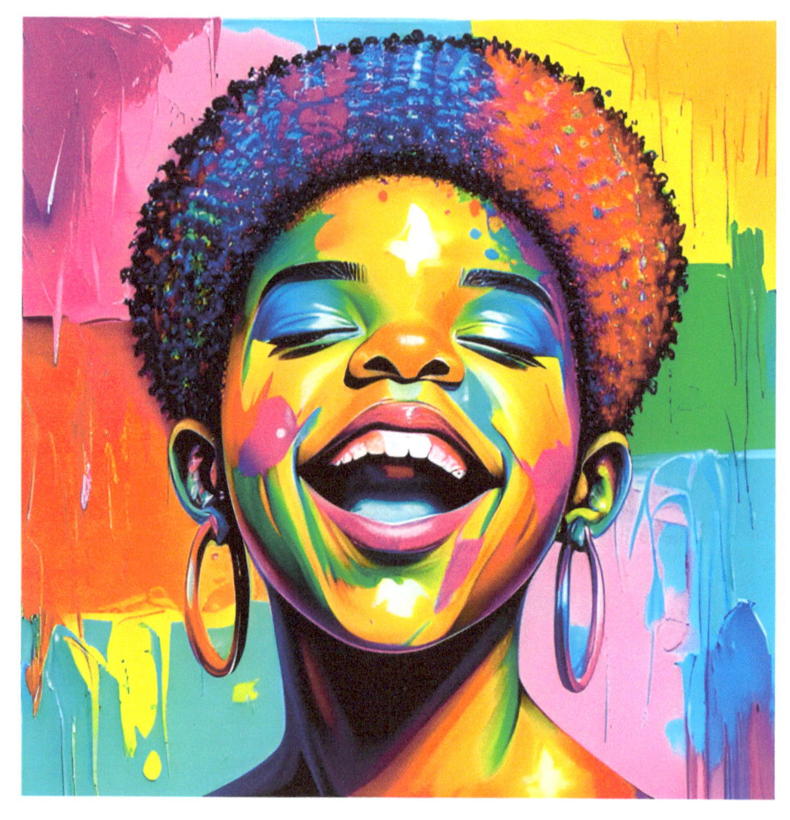

I make my ancestors proud daily.

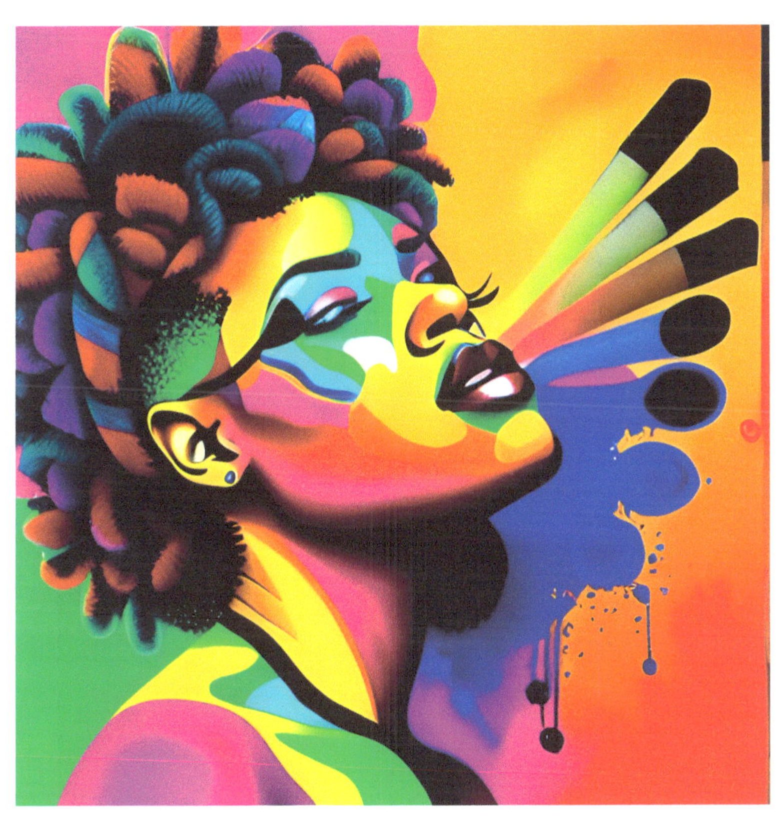

My attitude is fabulous and fierce.

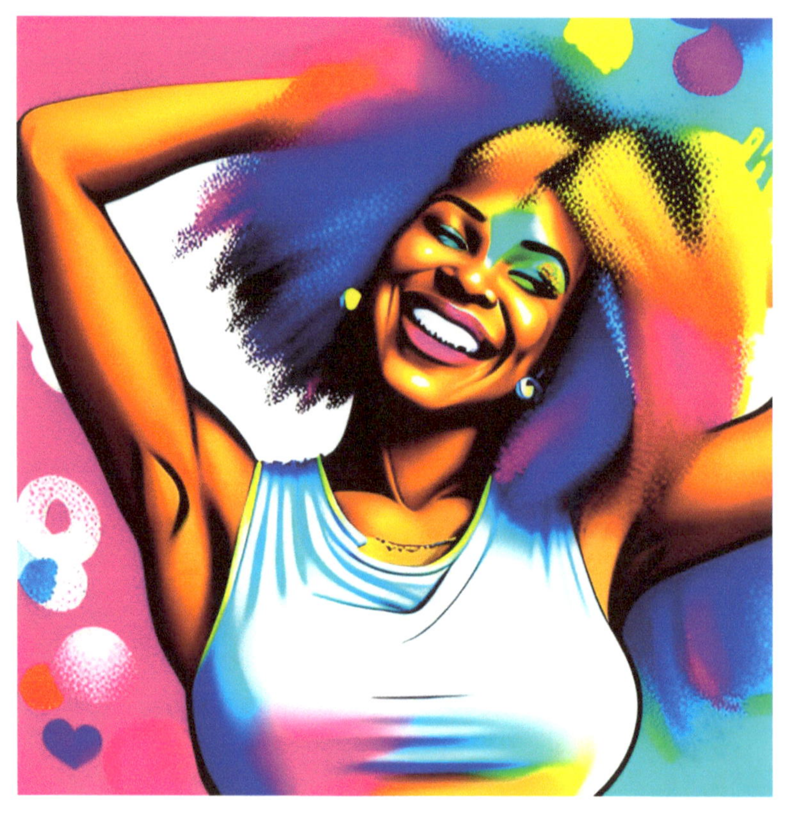

I am a supernatural being of love and light.

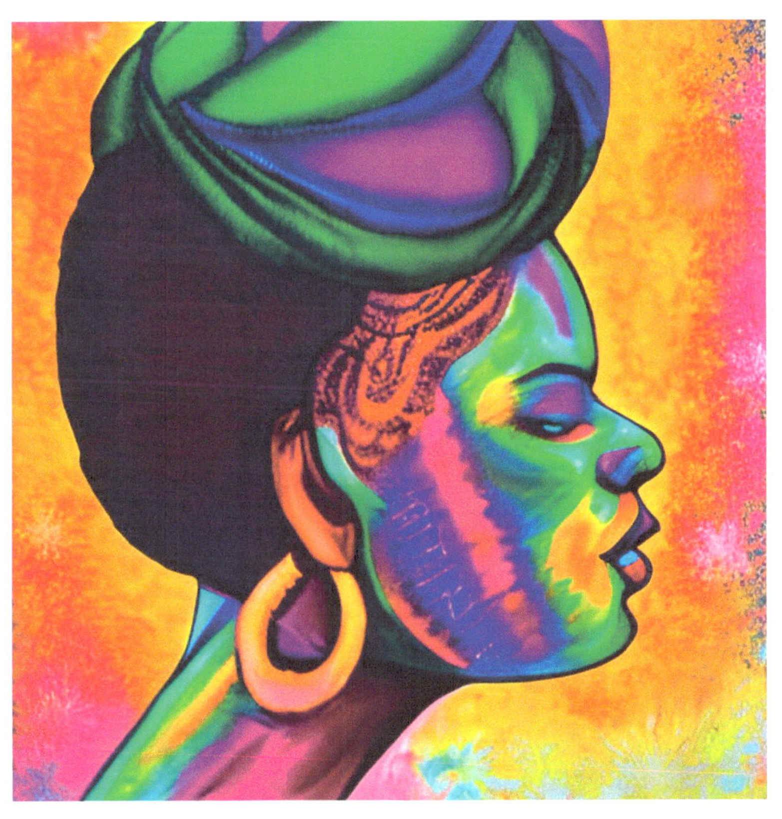

My roots make me strong.

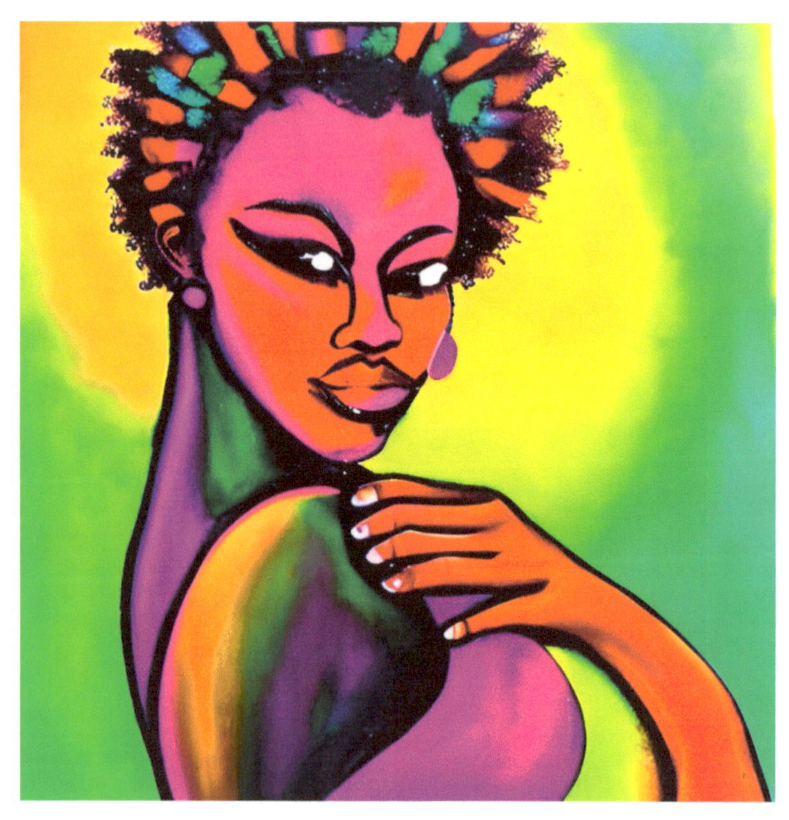

I am beautiful, inside and out.

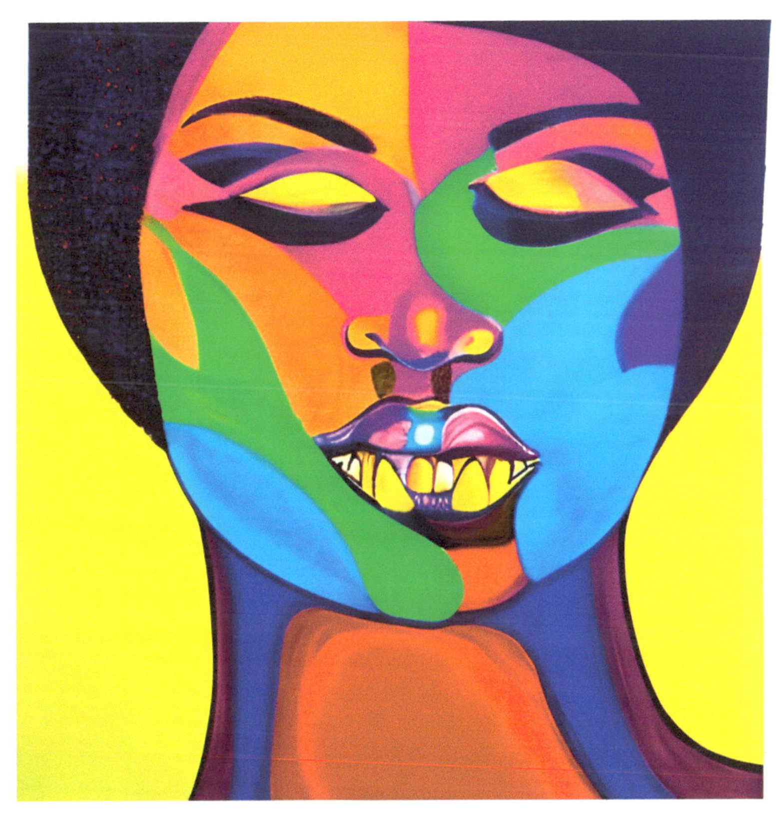

Everything about me is rich.

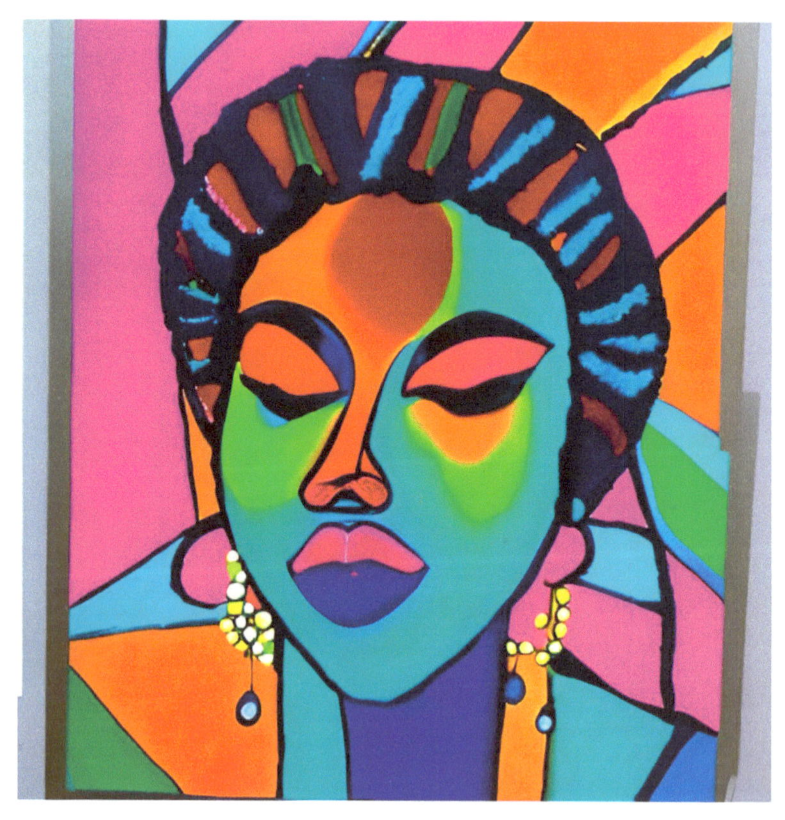

I am both classy and sassy.

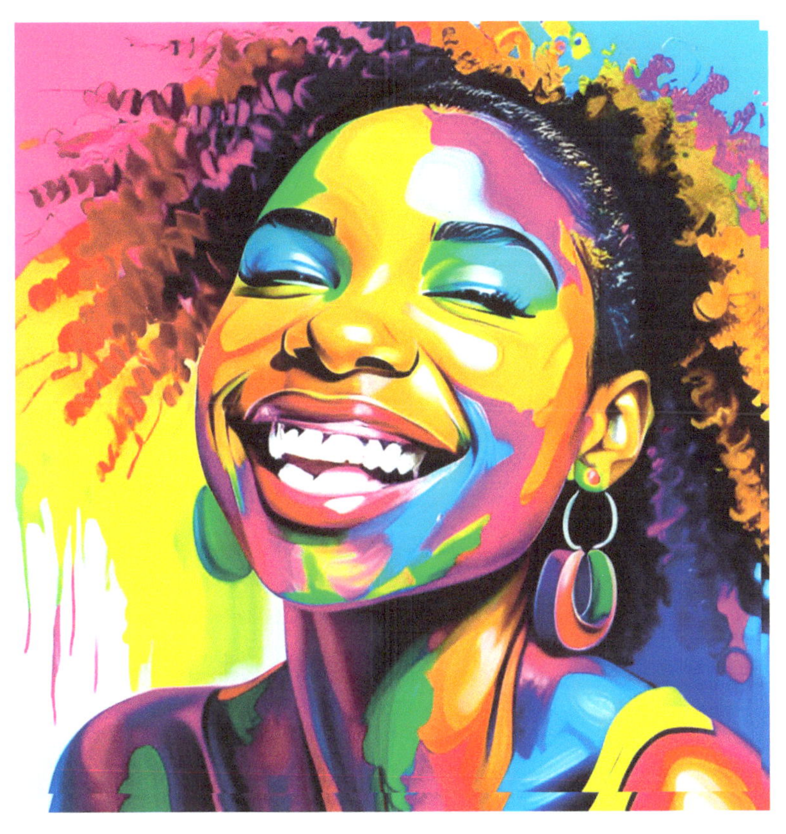

I accept and shine all of my colors.

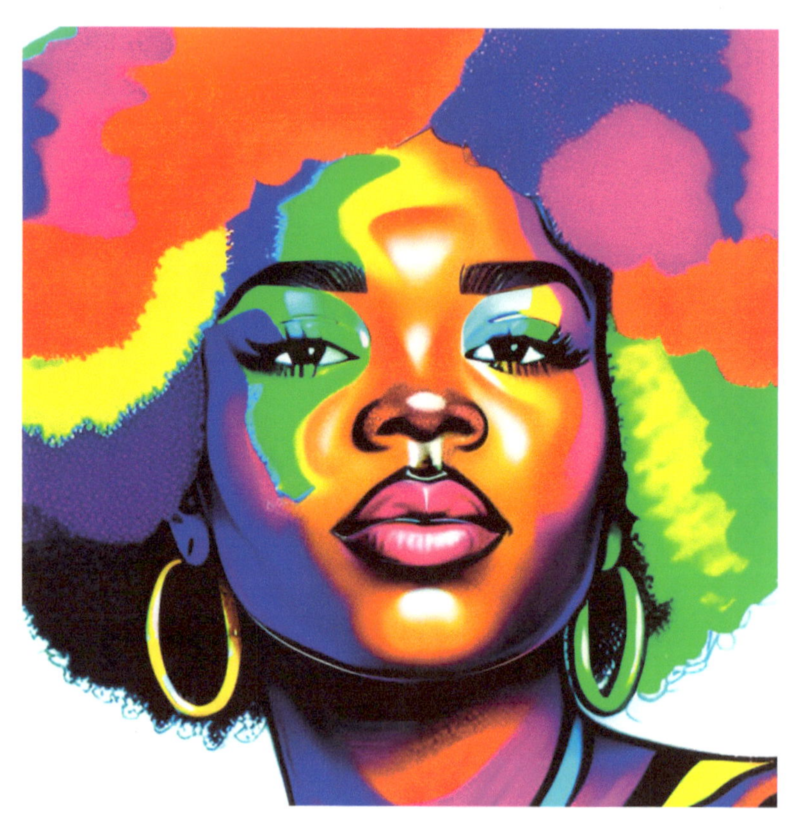

I am rare, one of a kind.

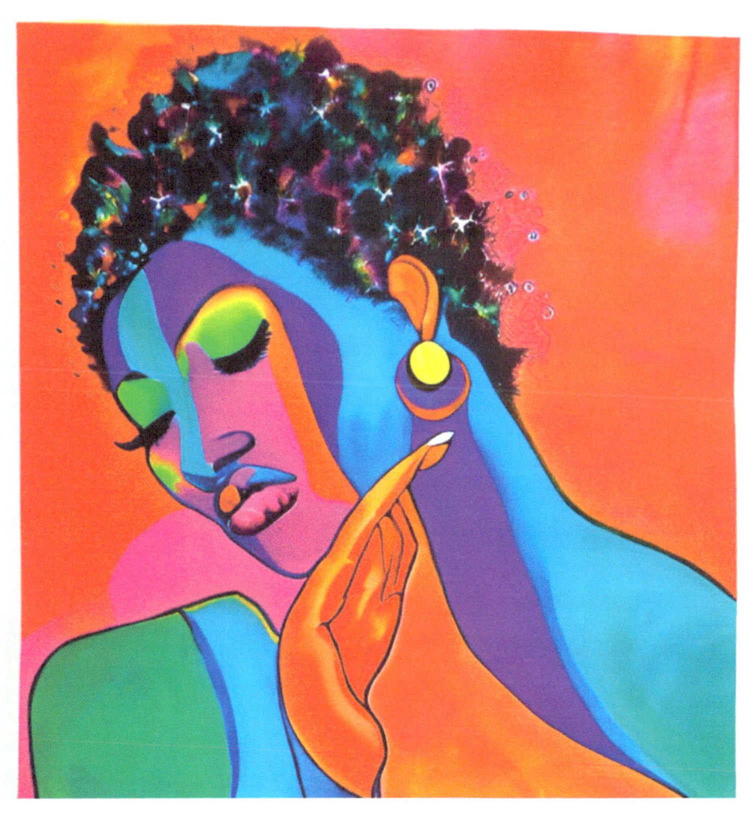

I don't sweat the small stuff.

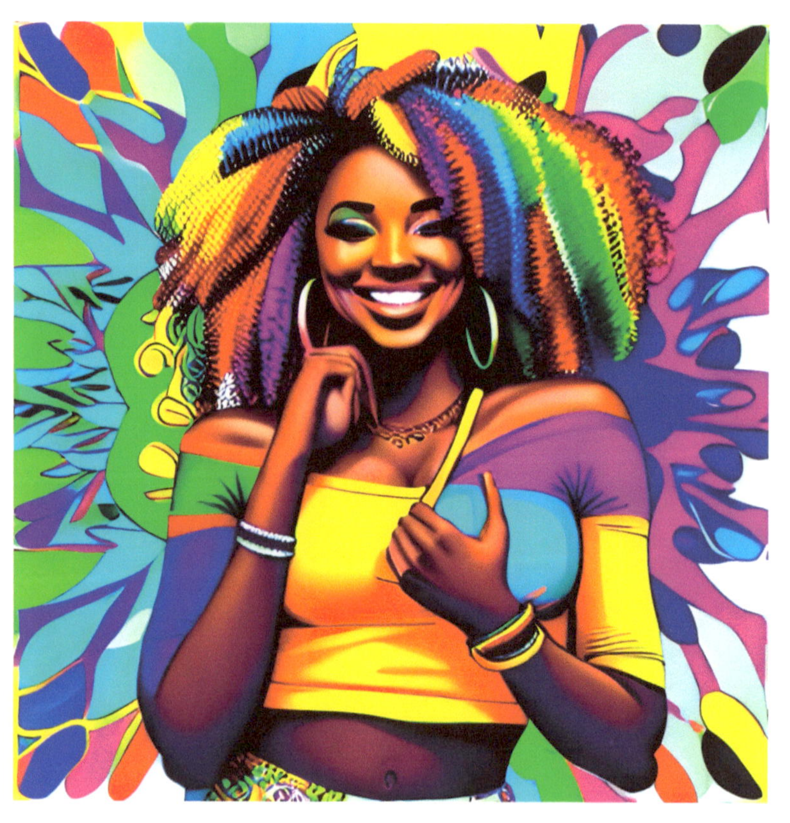

I attract wonderful things into my life.

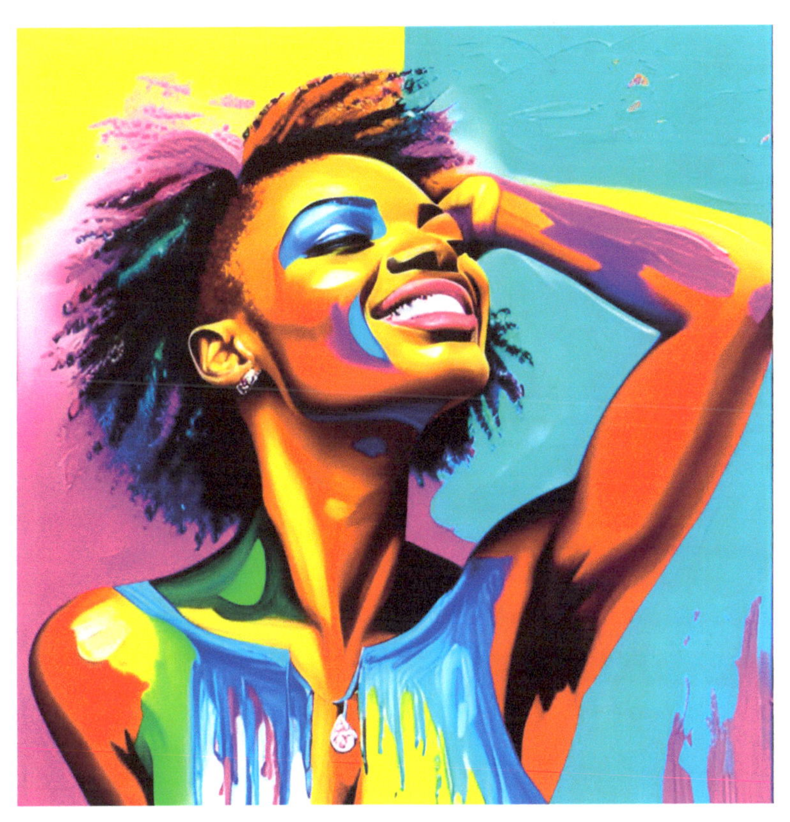

I nurture and love my body. My body is my soul's temple.

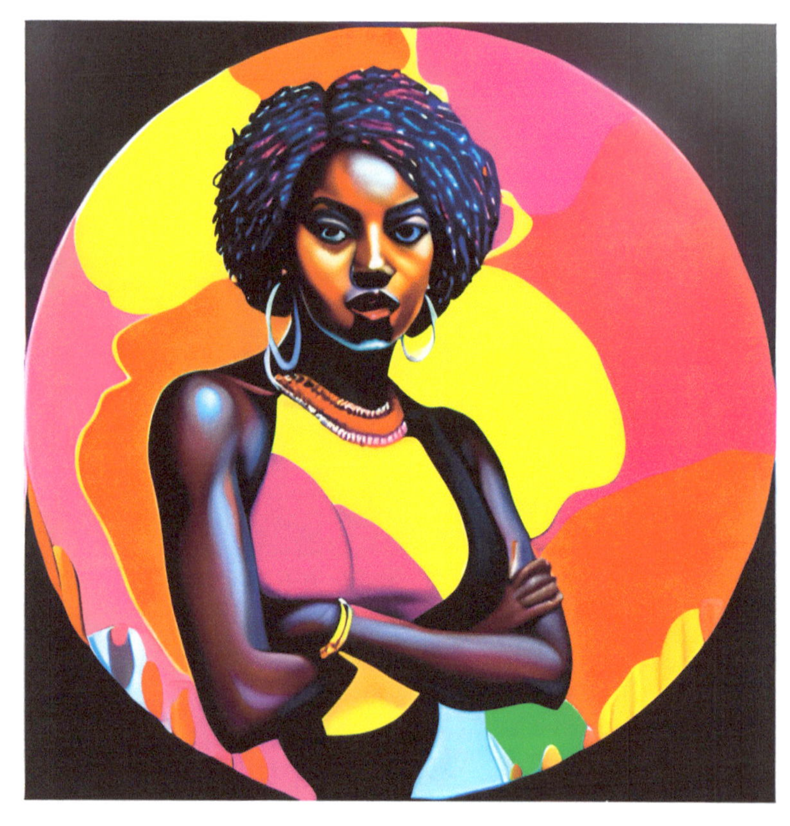

I have the courage to grow.

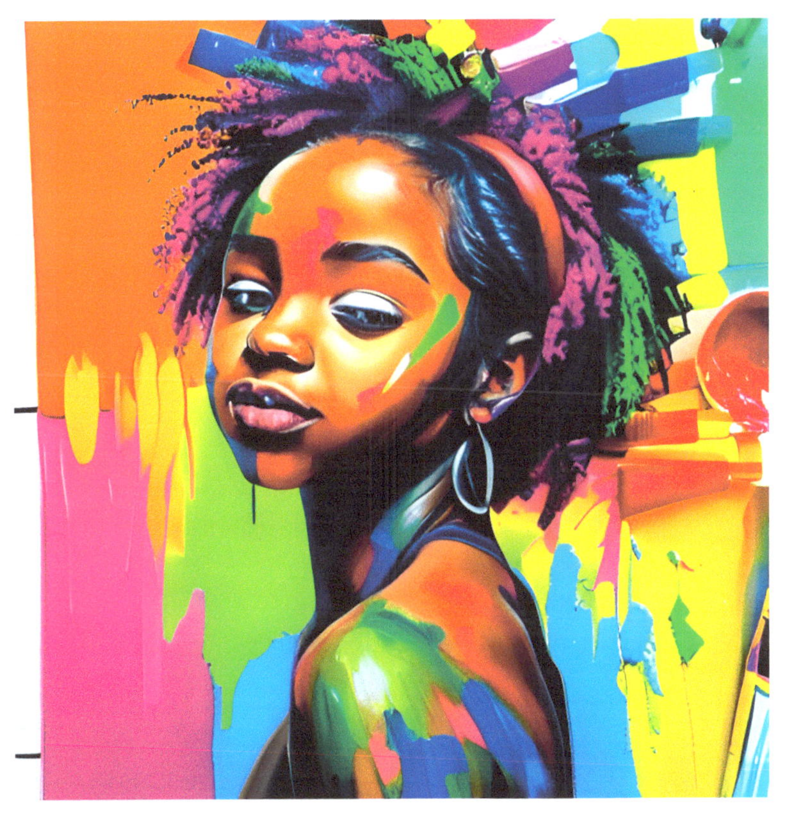

I work through my fears.

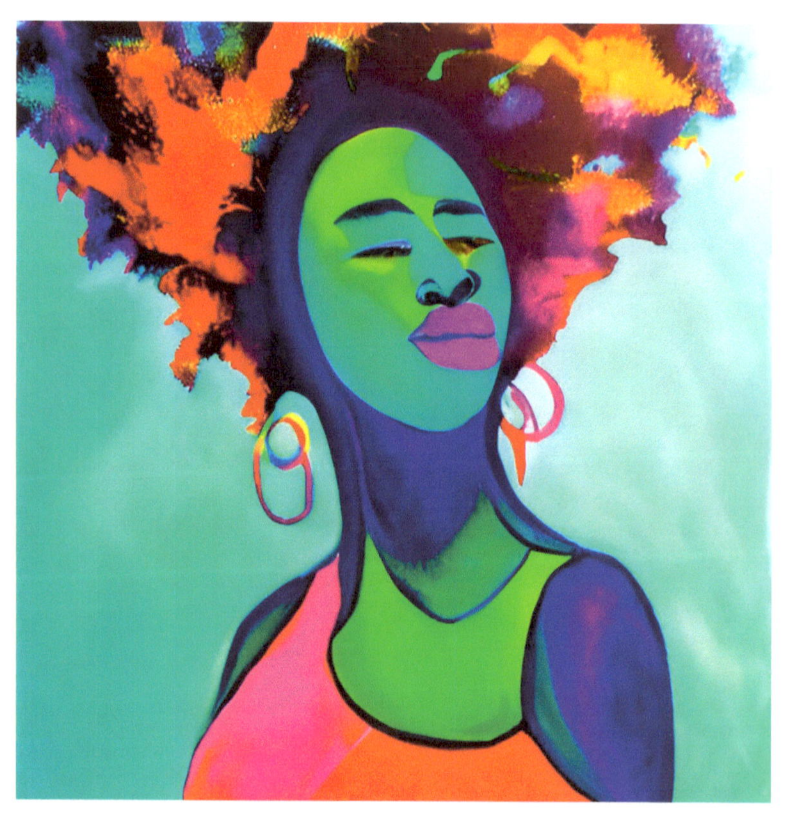

I appreciate life and all nature offers.

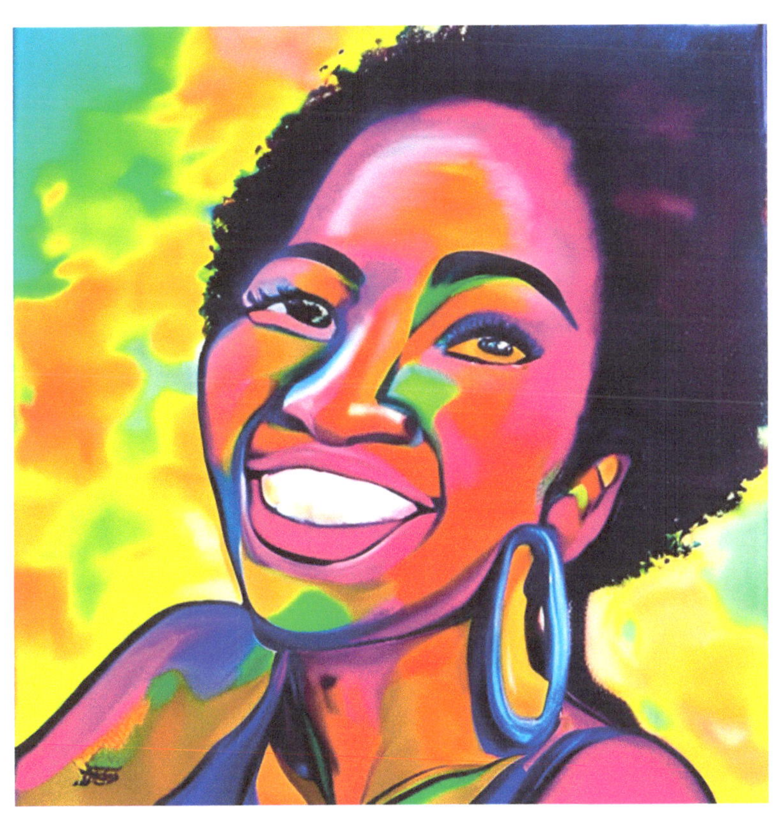

I can choose positivity daily.

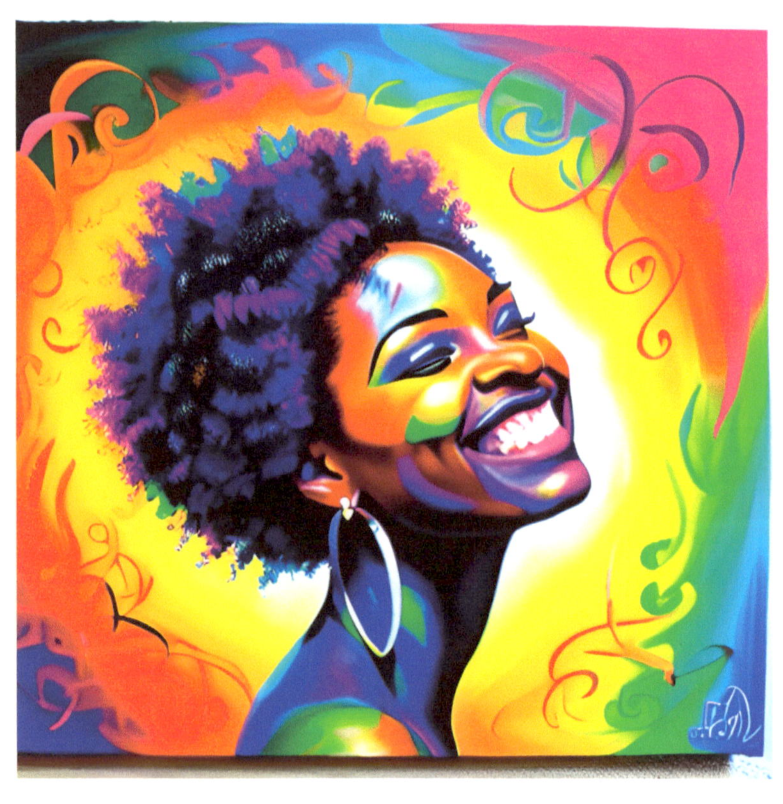

I am worthy of success.

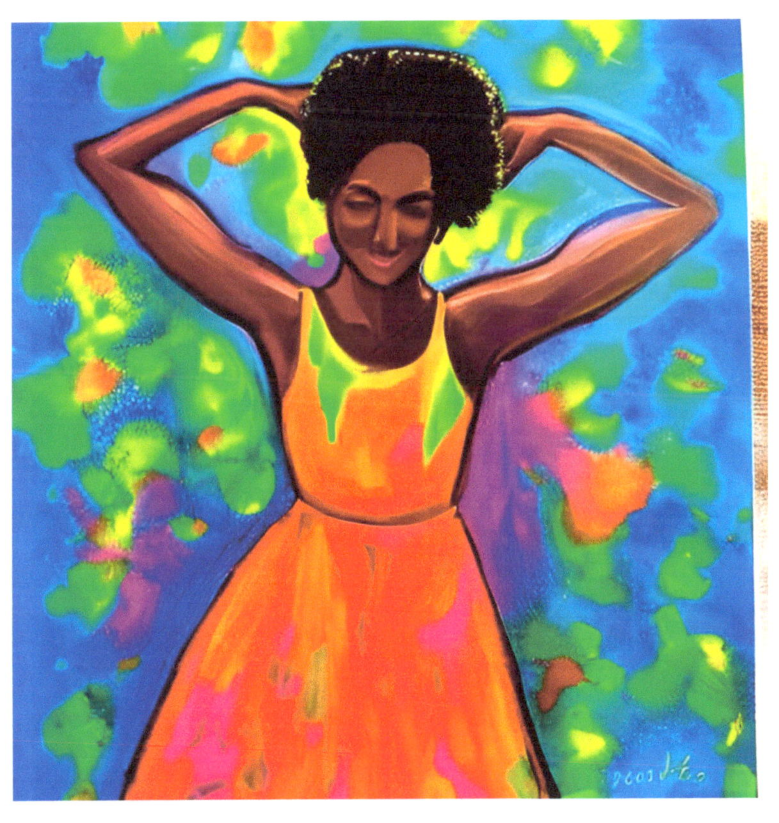

Like a favorite song, I am timeless.

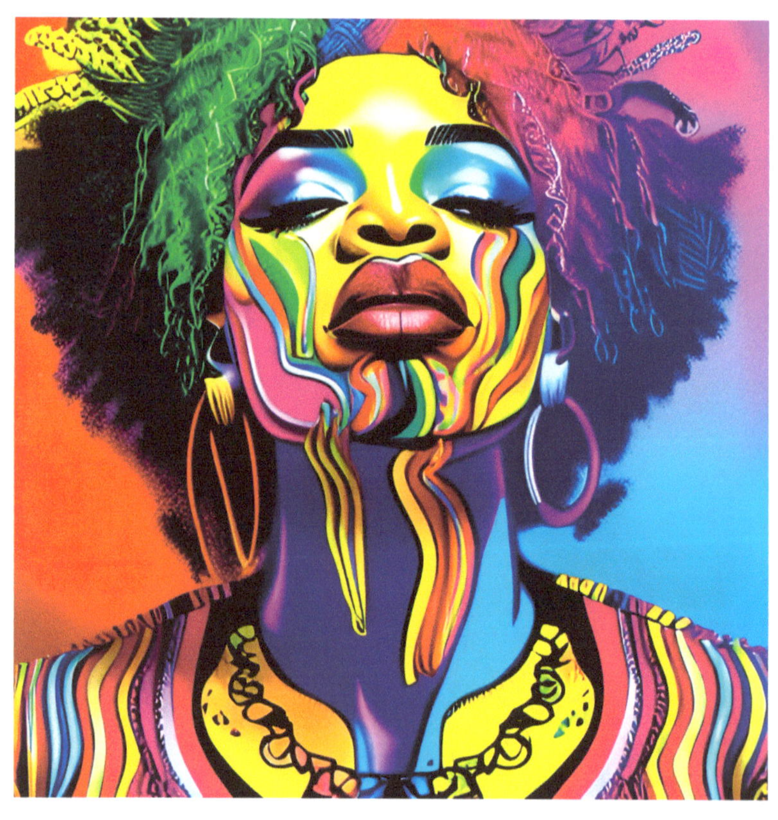

I am the Vibe.

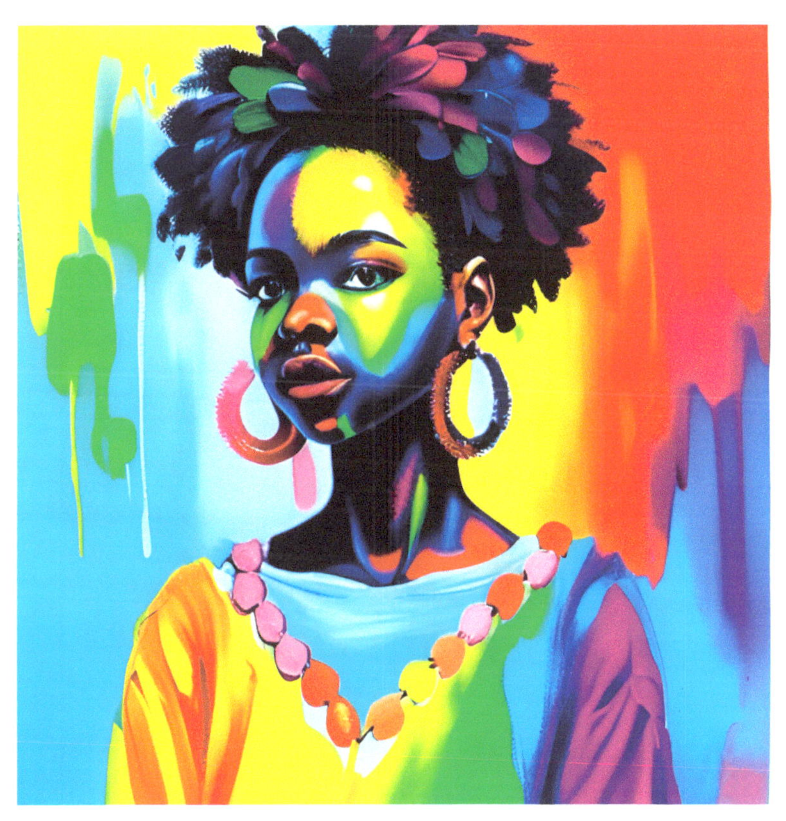

I learn from my mistakes.

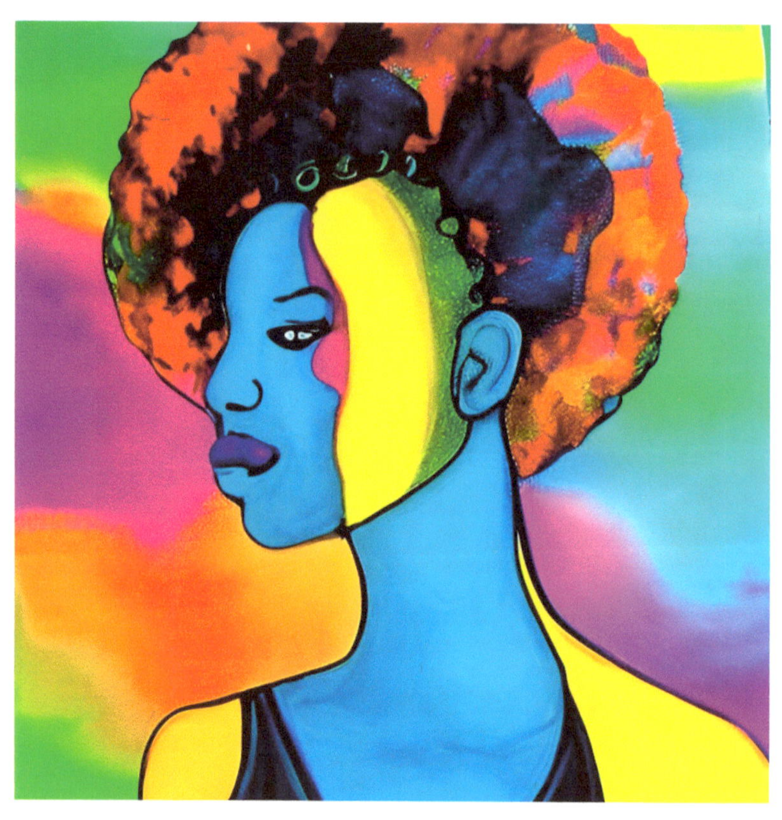

My wounds heal.

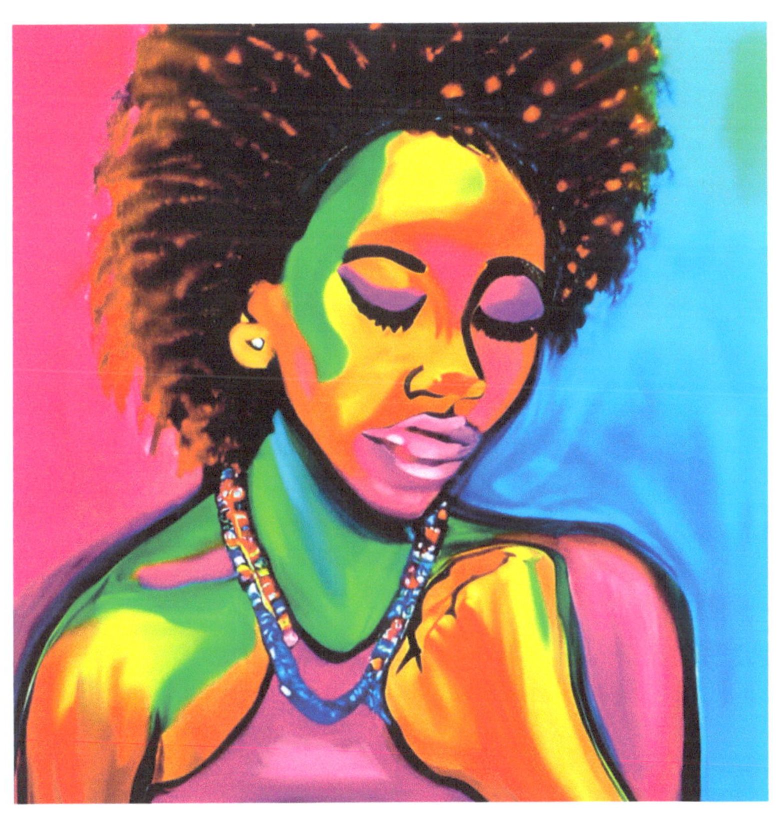

I am calm and collected, even when under pressure.

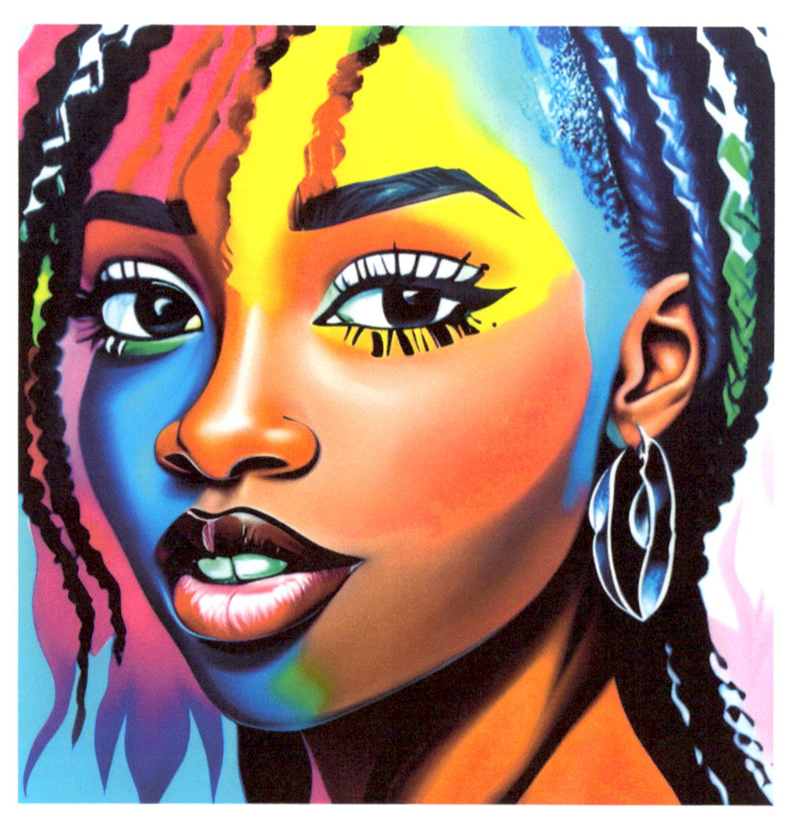

I am unique.
My differences make
me special.

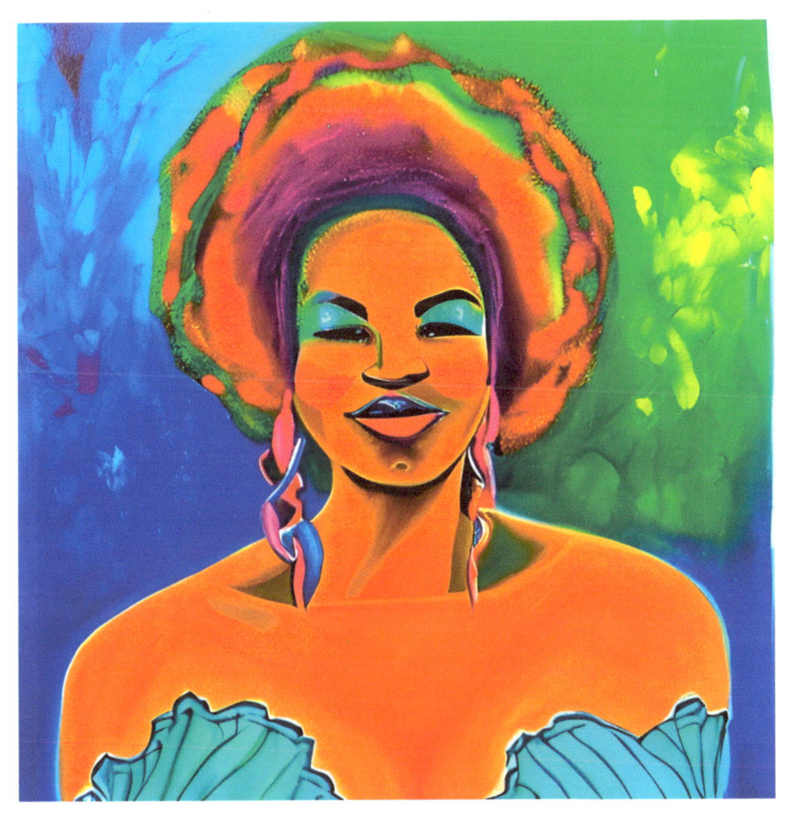

I flow with life. Everything comes to pass.

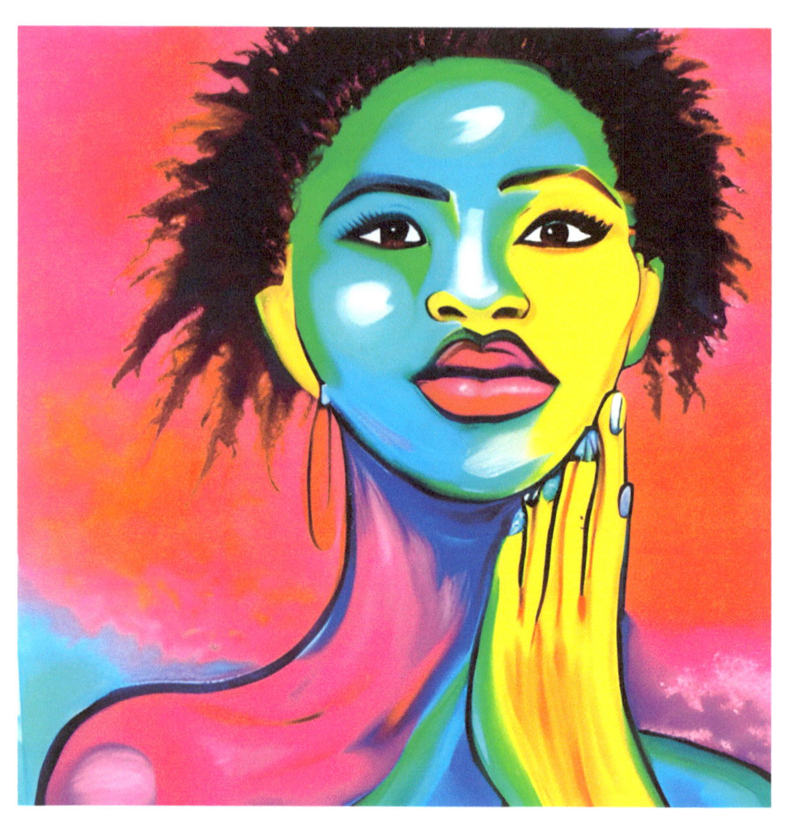

I am freedom.

Watch me shine.

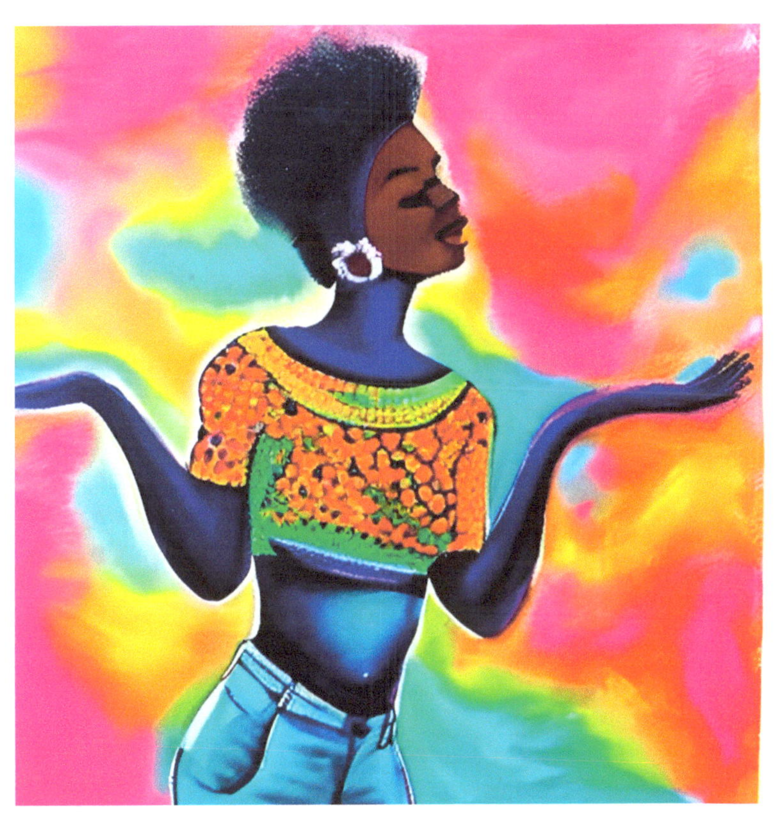

I am vibrant and youthful.

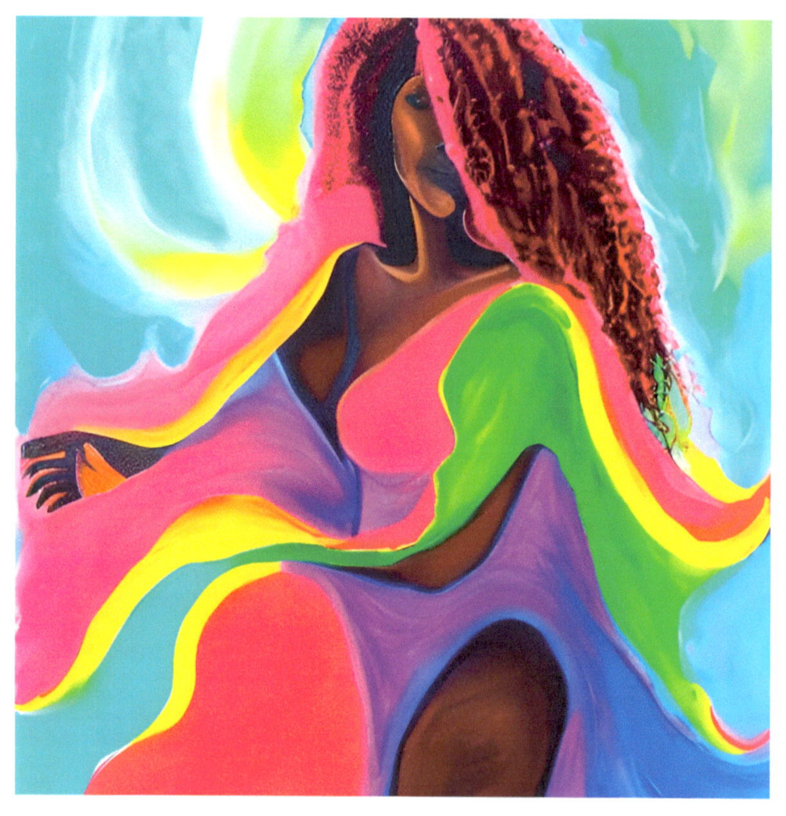

I am power with grace.

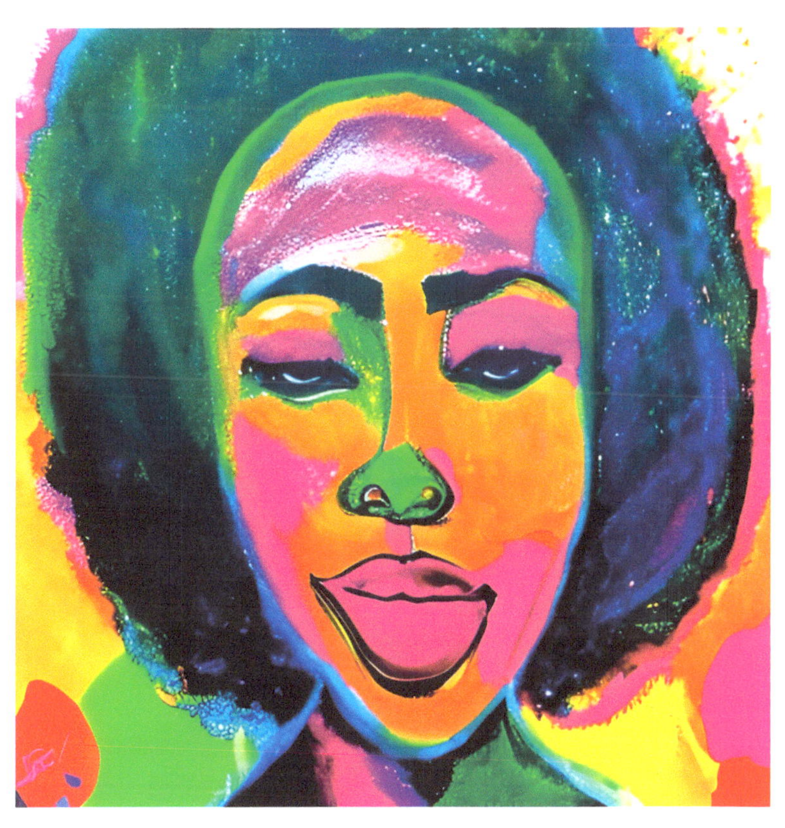

I am wise because I am self-aware.

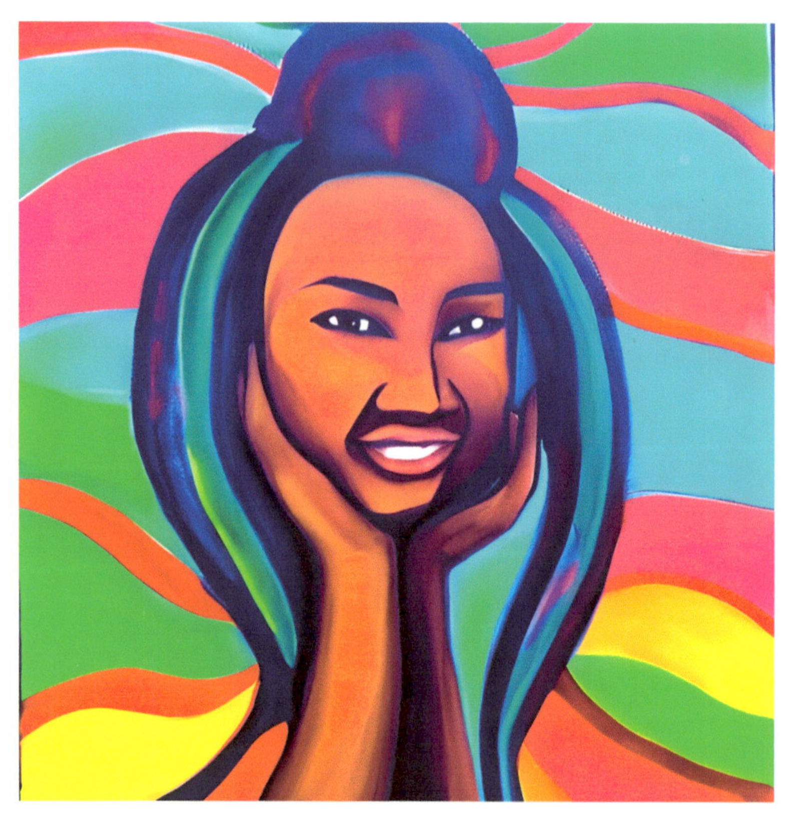

I can be the hero in my story.

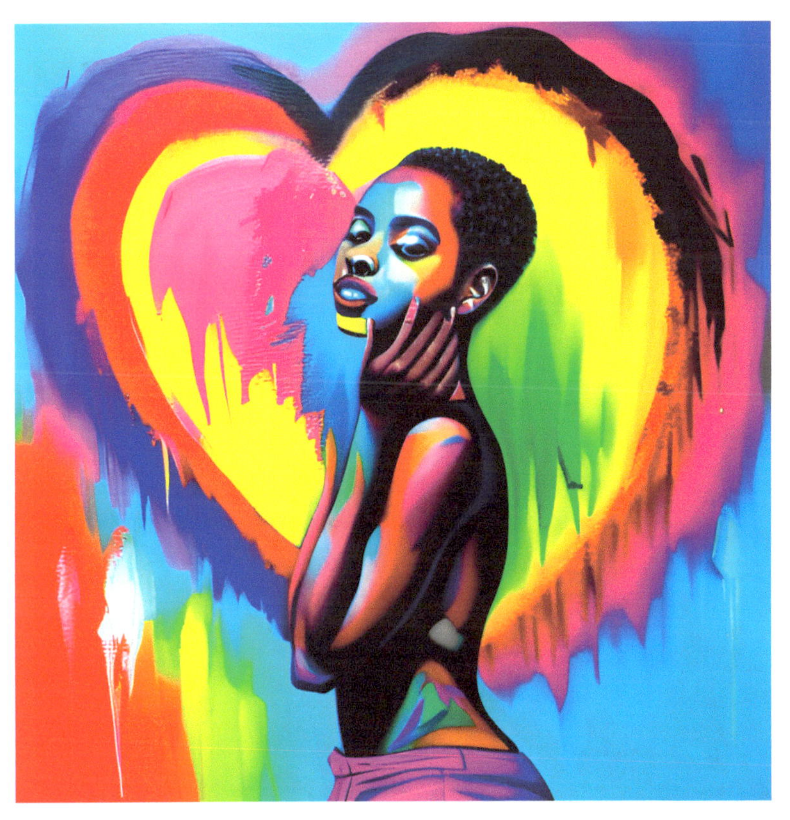

I teach people how I want to be treated.

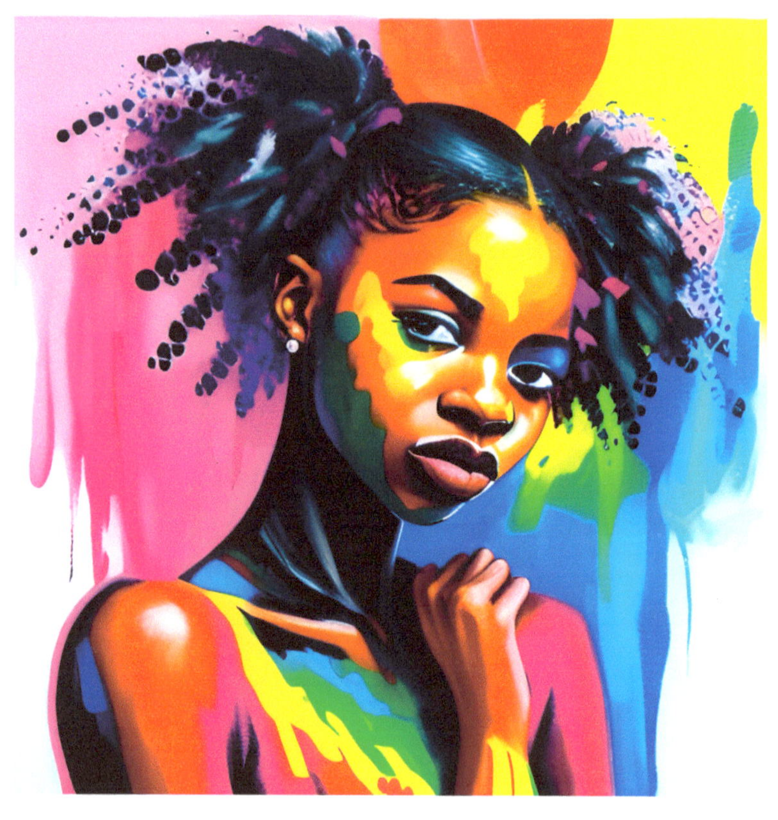

I stand up for what's right, even if I stand alone.

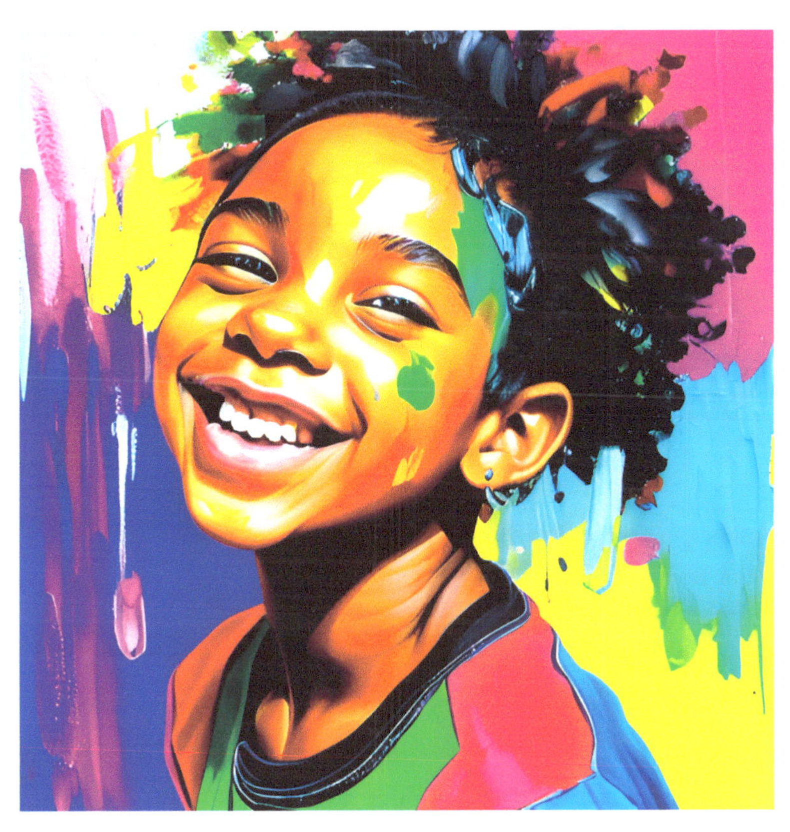

I am always looking to learn.

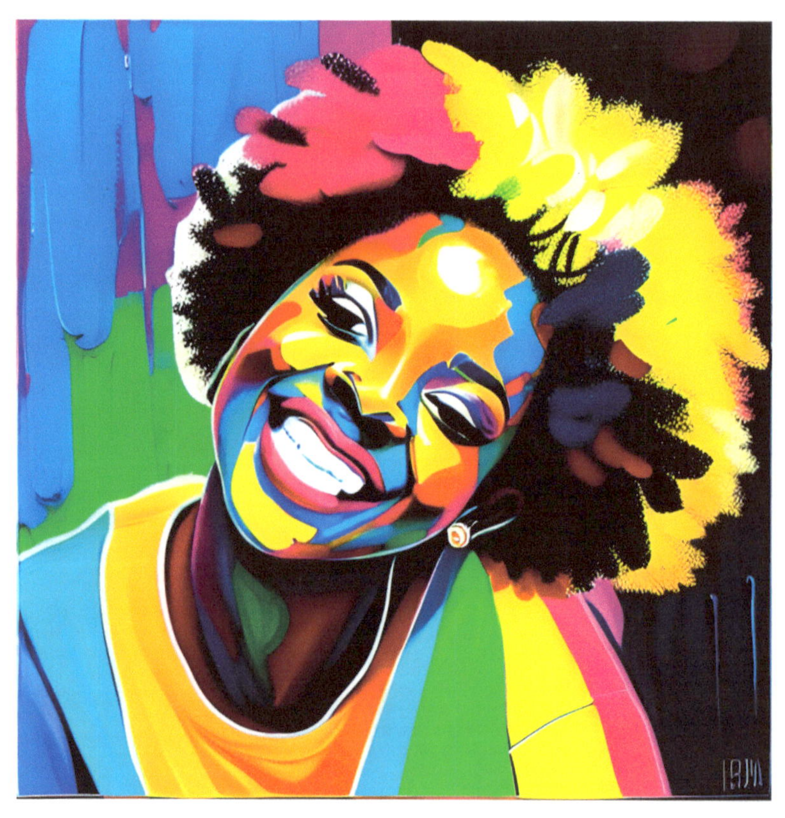

I am joy living to express myself.

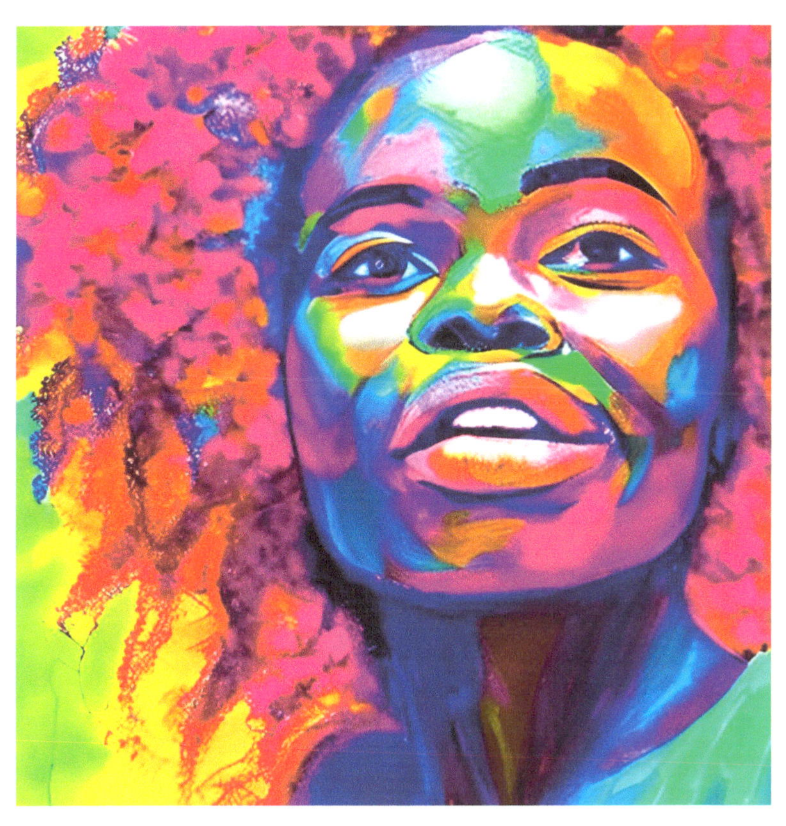

I am the change I wish to see in the world.

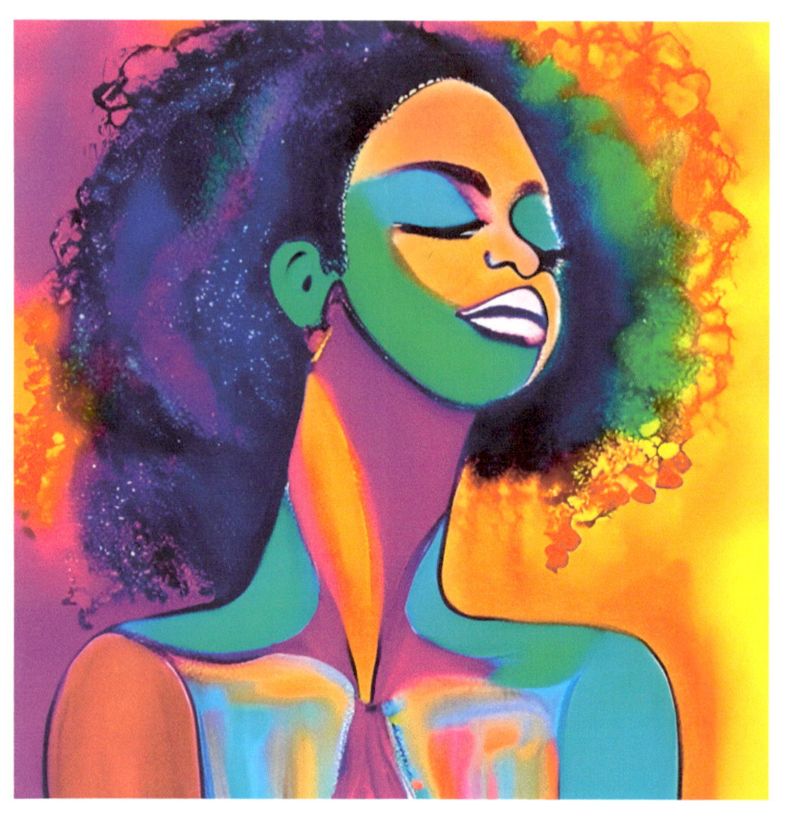

I am the future.

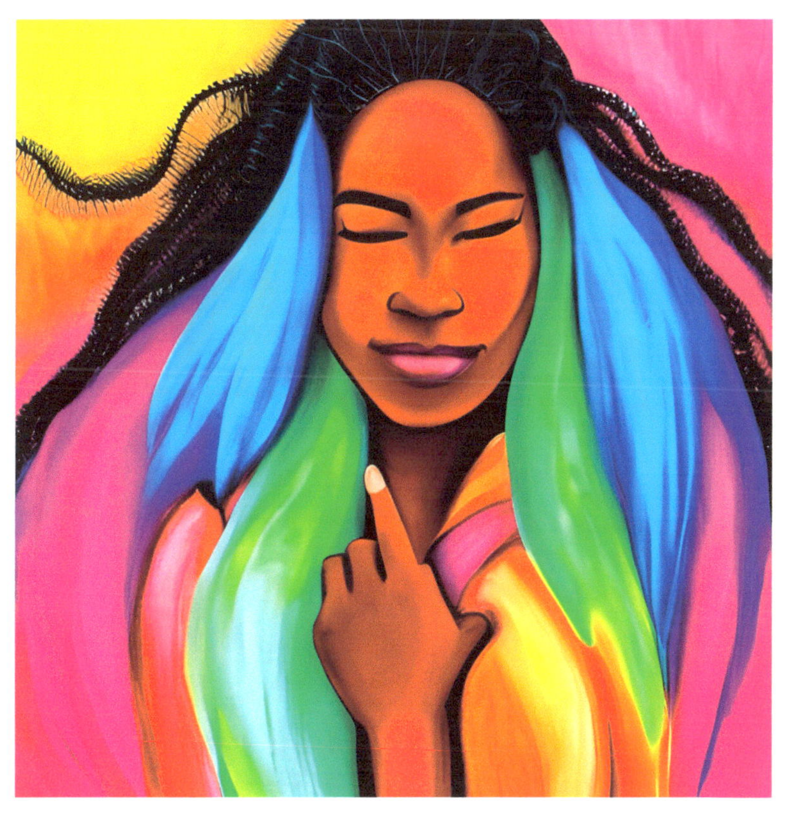

I am present.

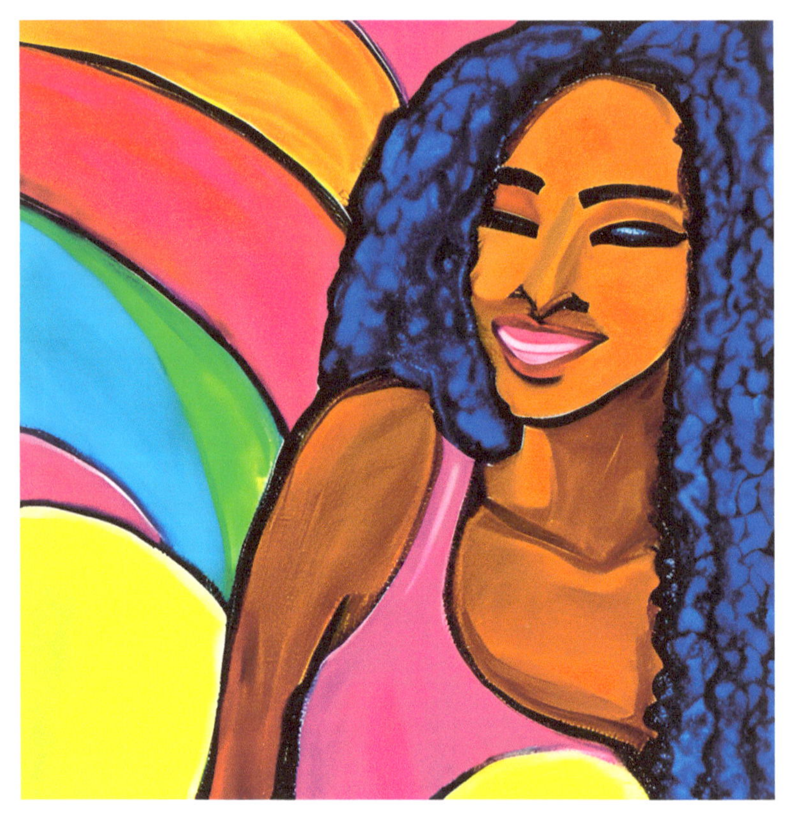

I am authentically and unapologetically me.

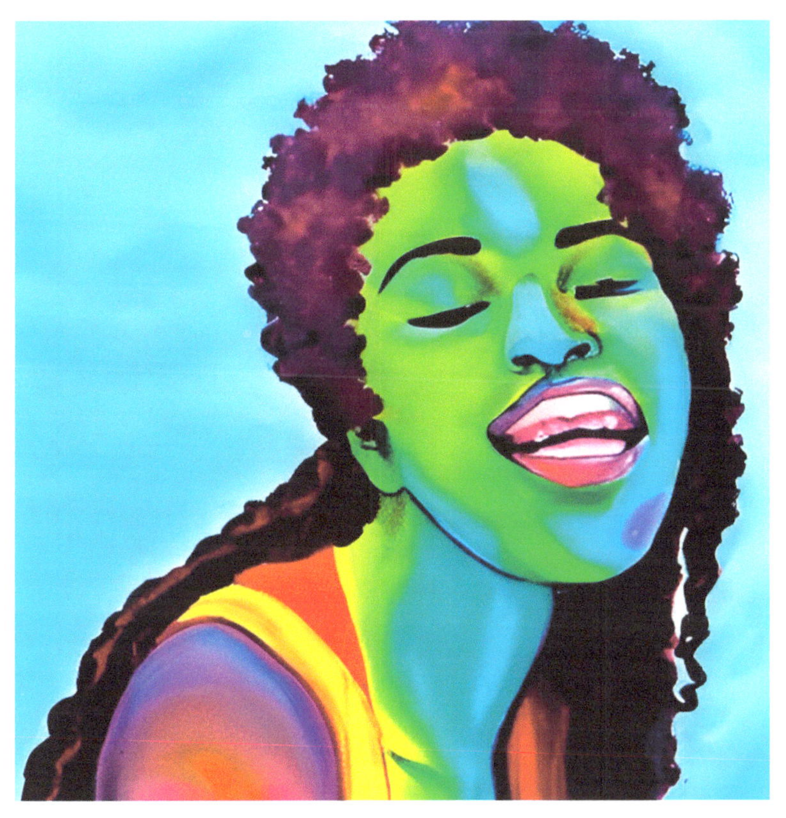

I am safe.

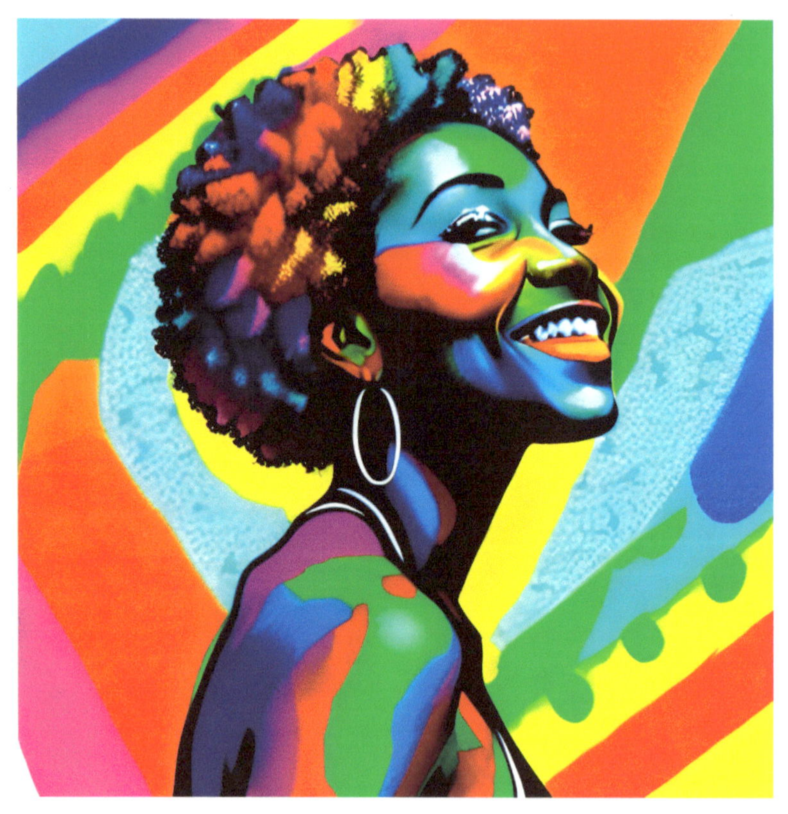

I am clever and cool.

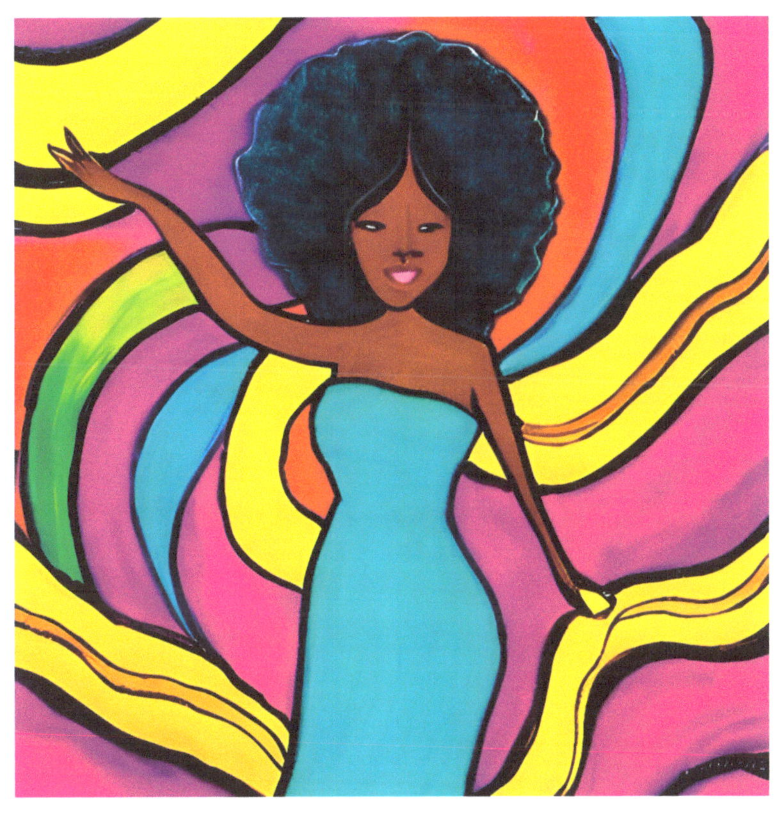

I am music that makes your soul groove.

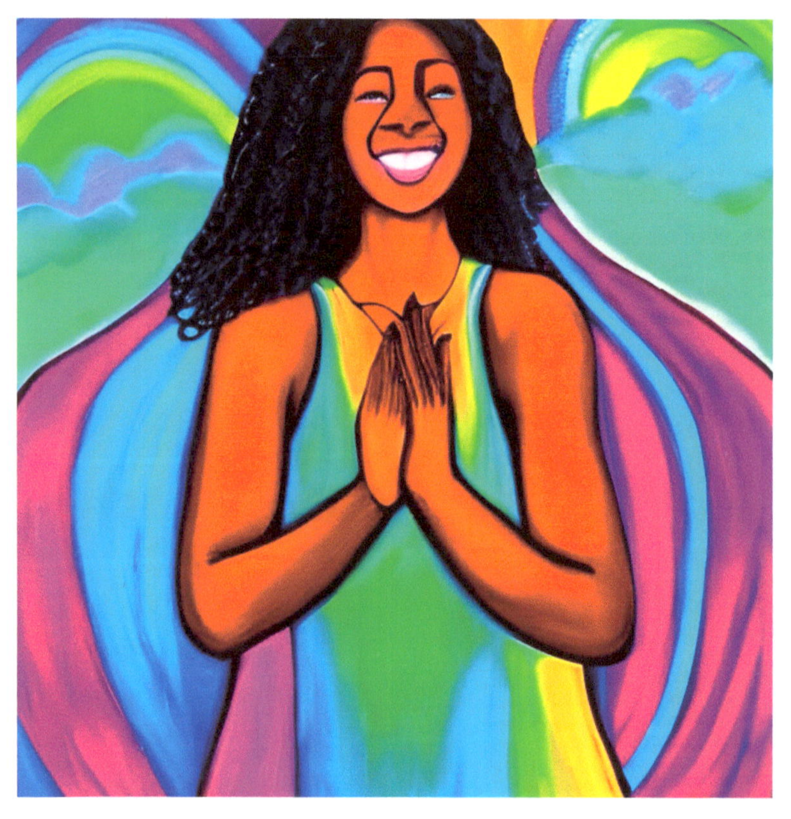

I am growing daily.

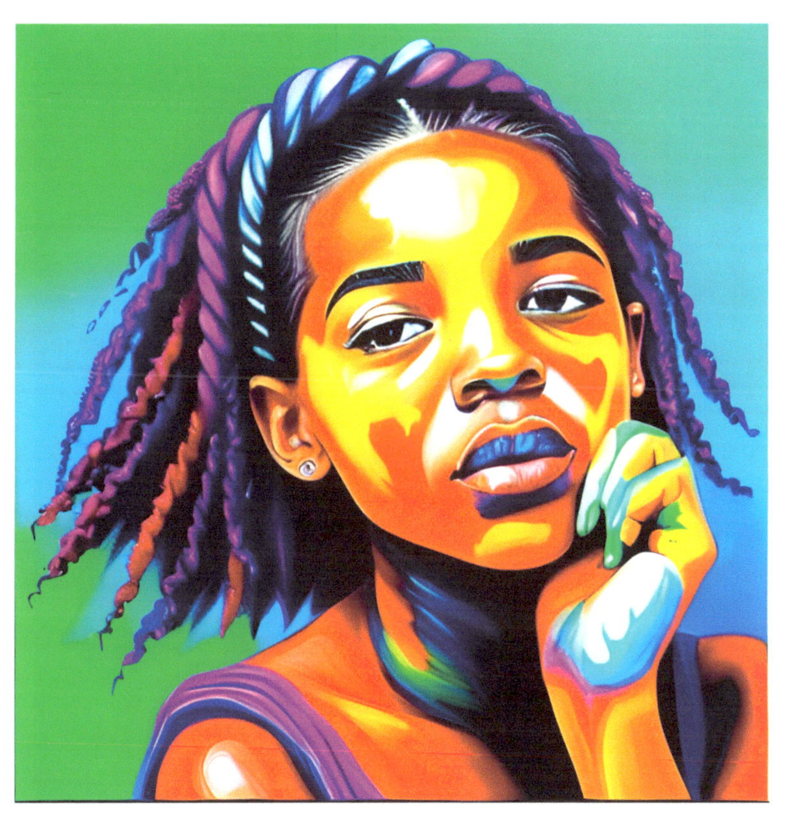

I don't give up easily.

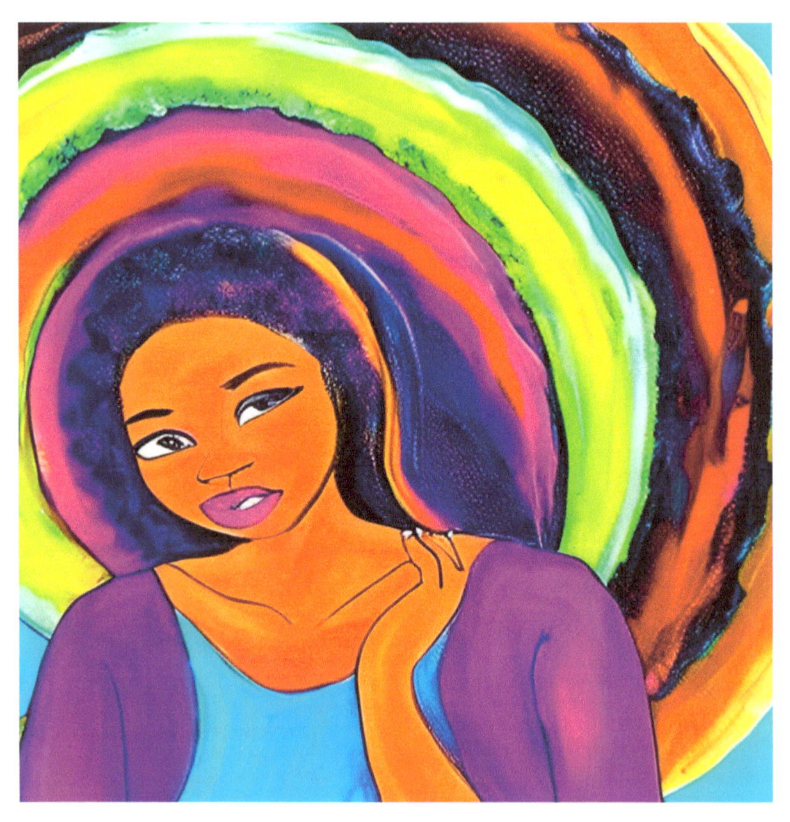

I am more than my passing thoughts.

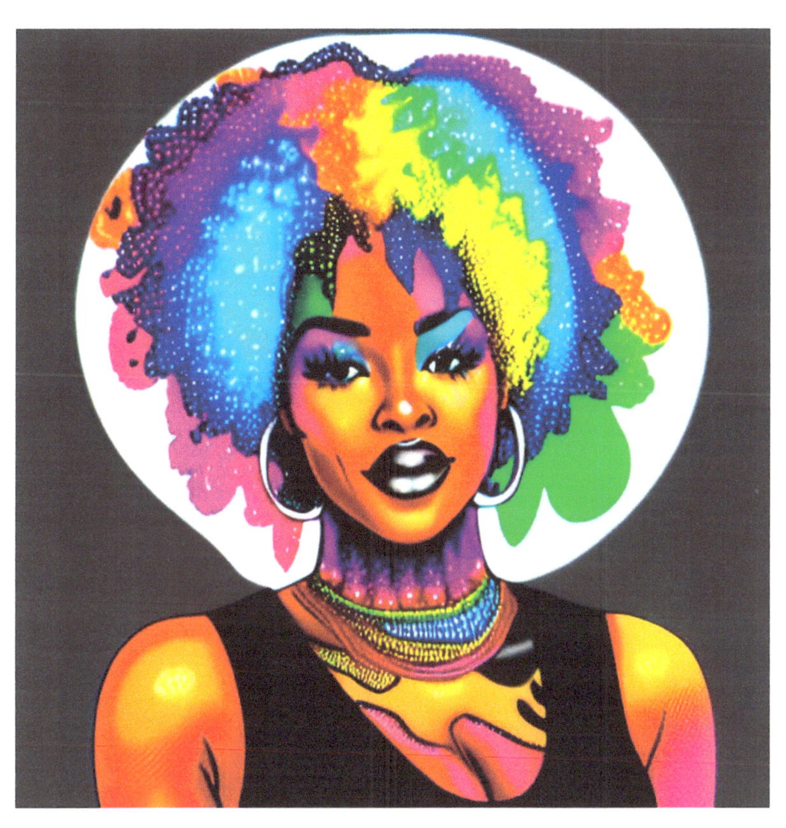

I am responsible for my actions.

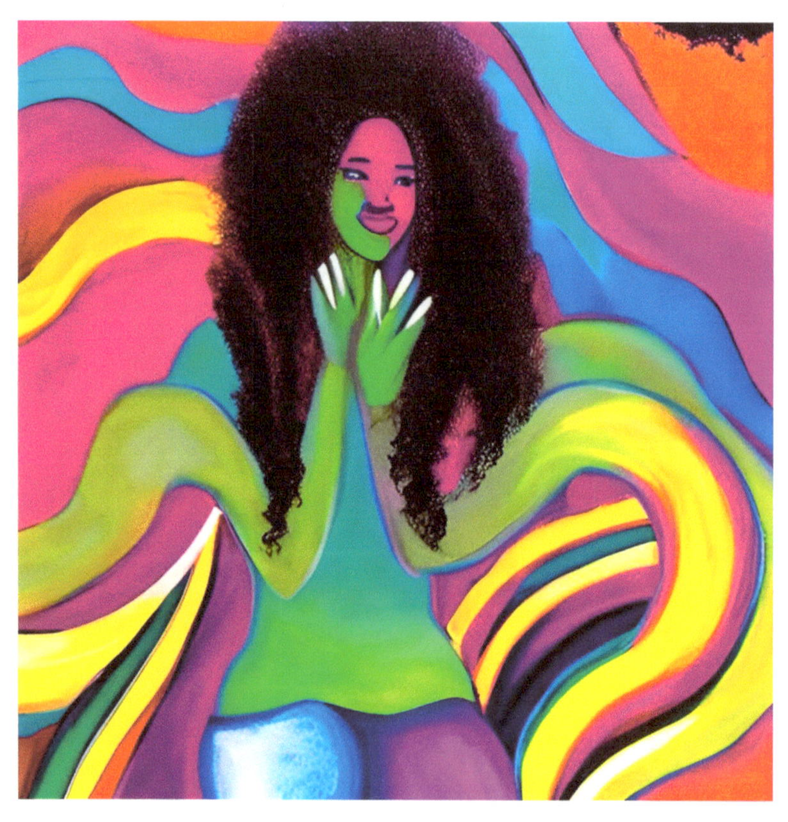

I attract money and wealth.

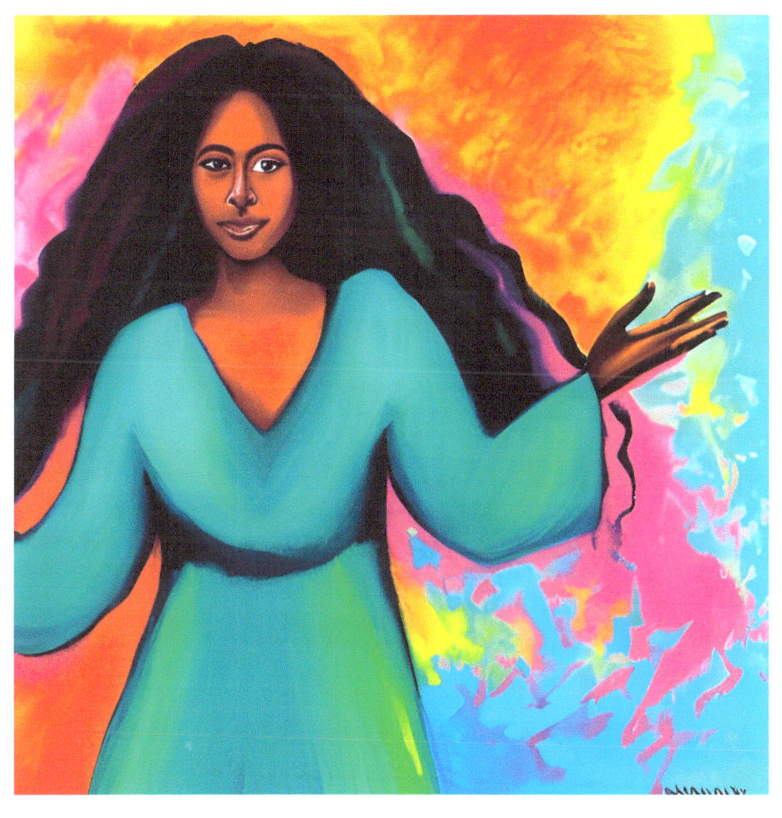

I am a creative creator.

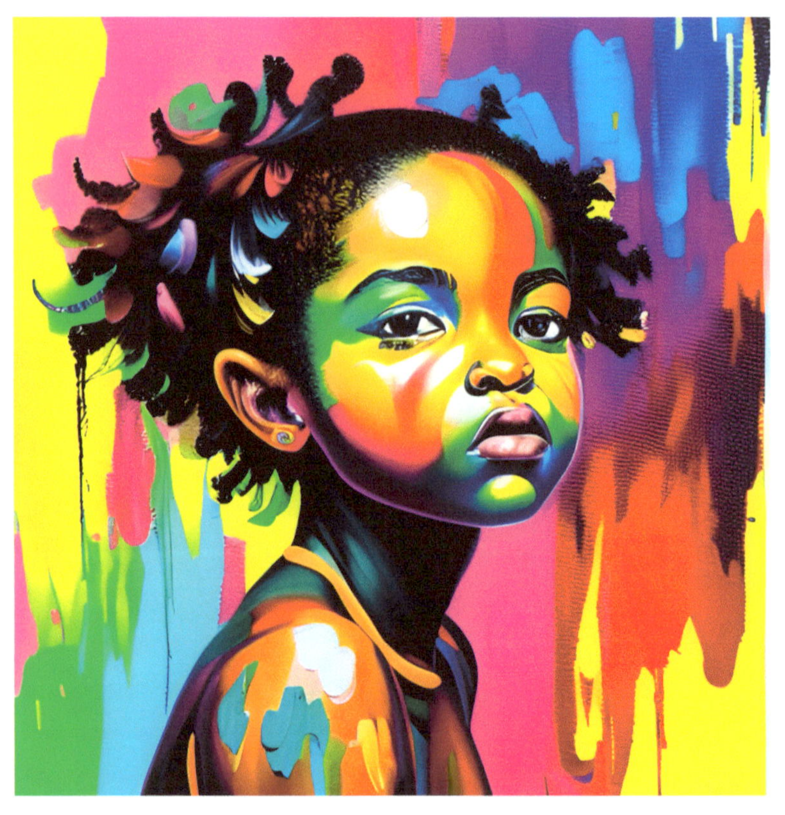

I have purpose.

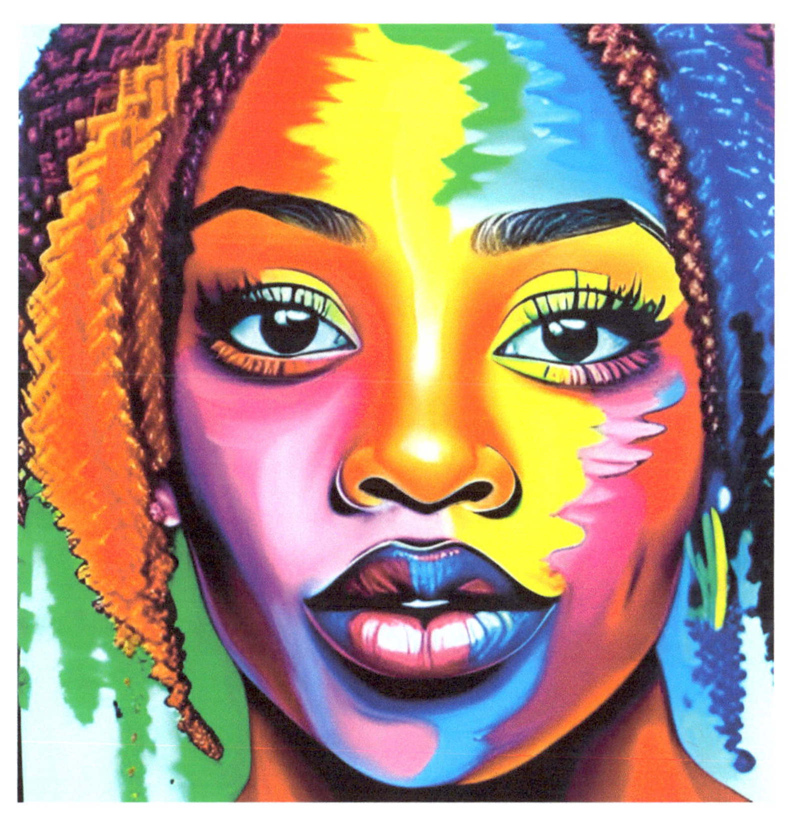

I am meant for greatness.

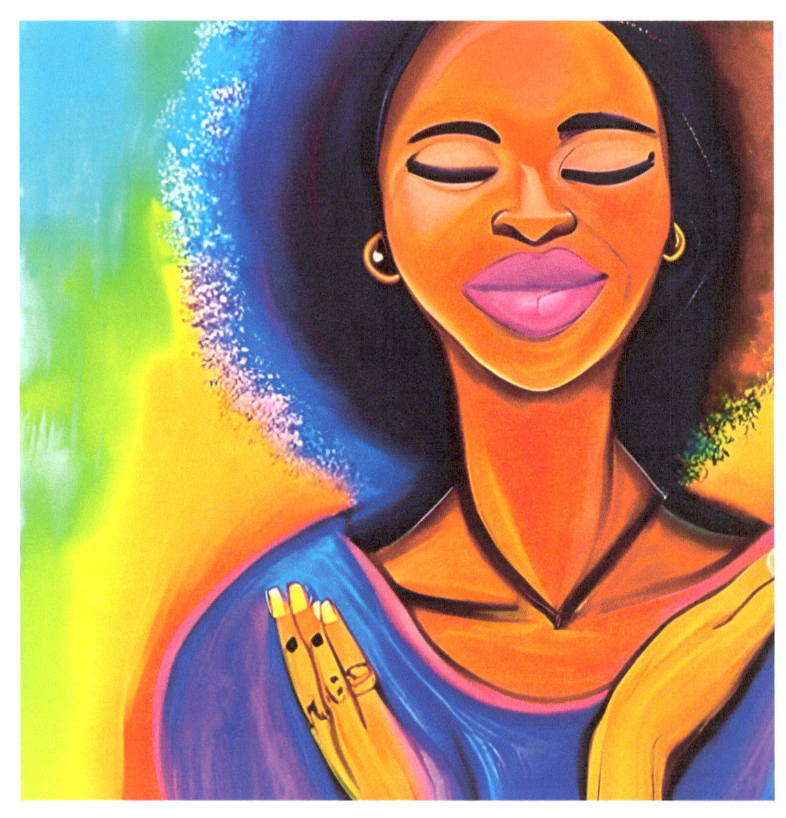

I am supported in my dreams.

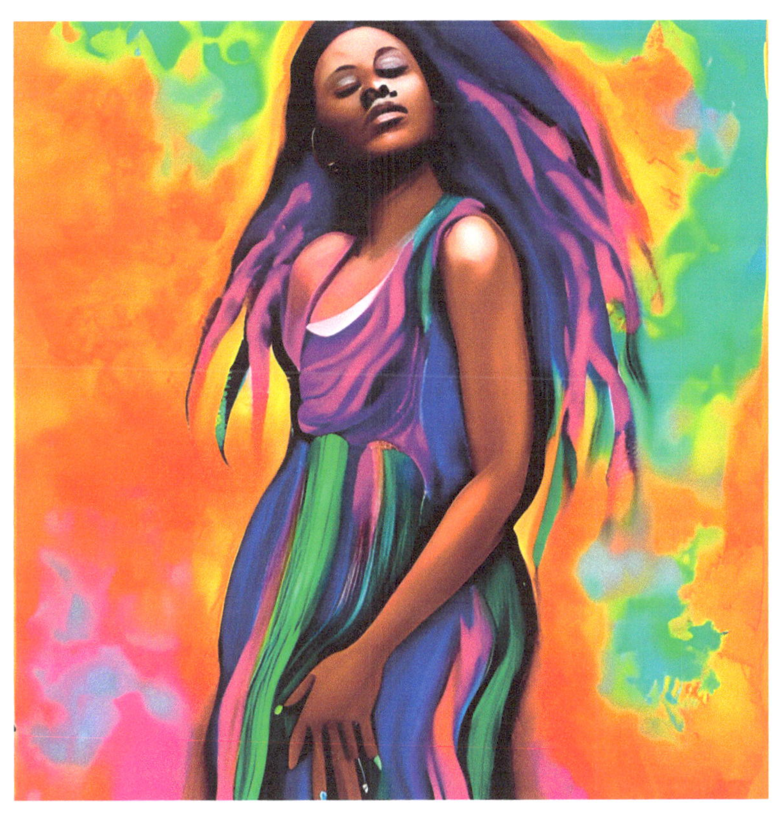

I have the determination to achieve.

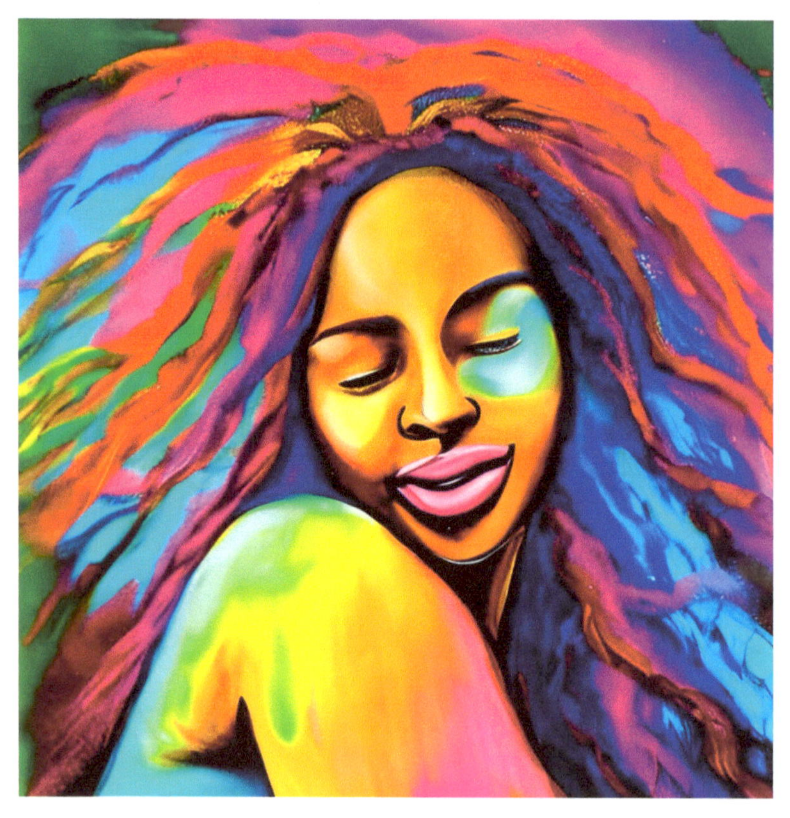

I embrace change.

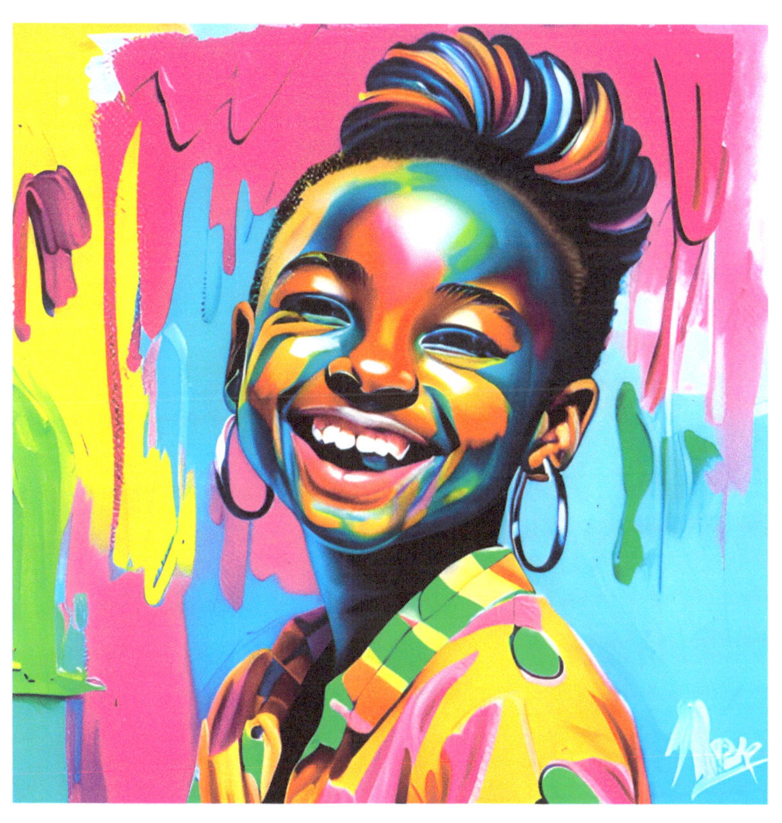

I am protected.

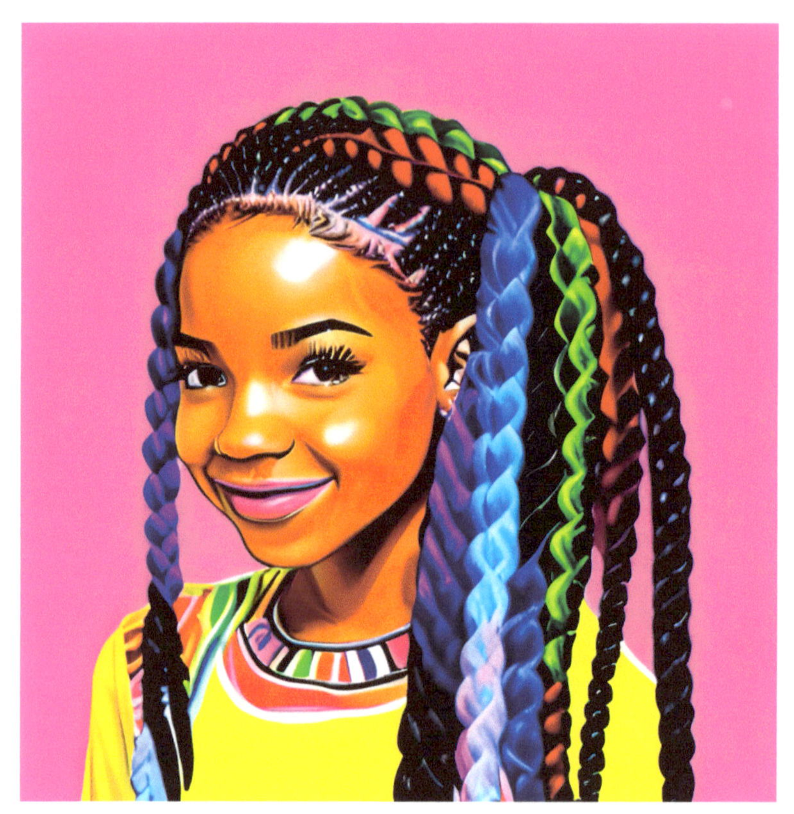

I matter.

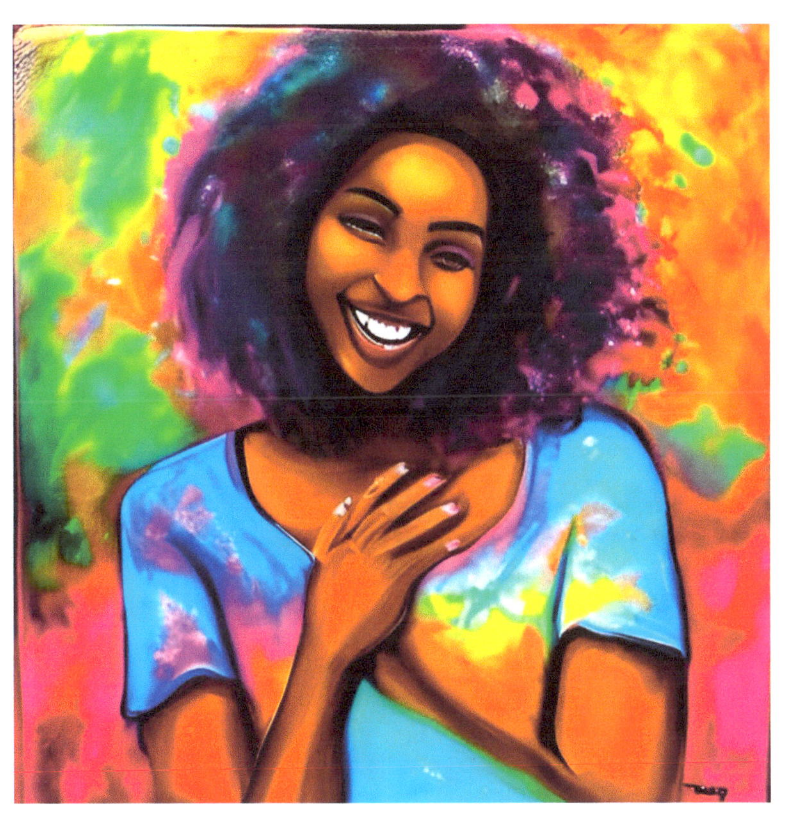

I believe in myself and that drives me.

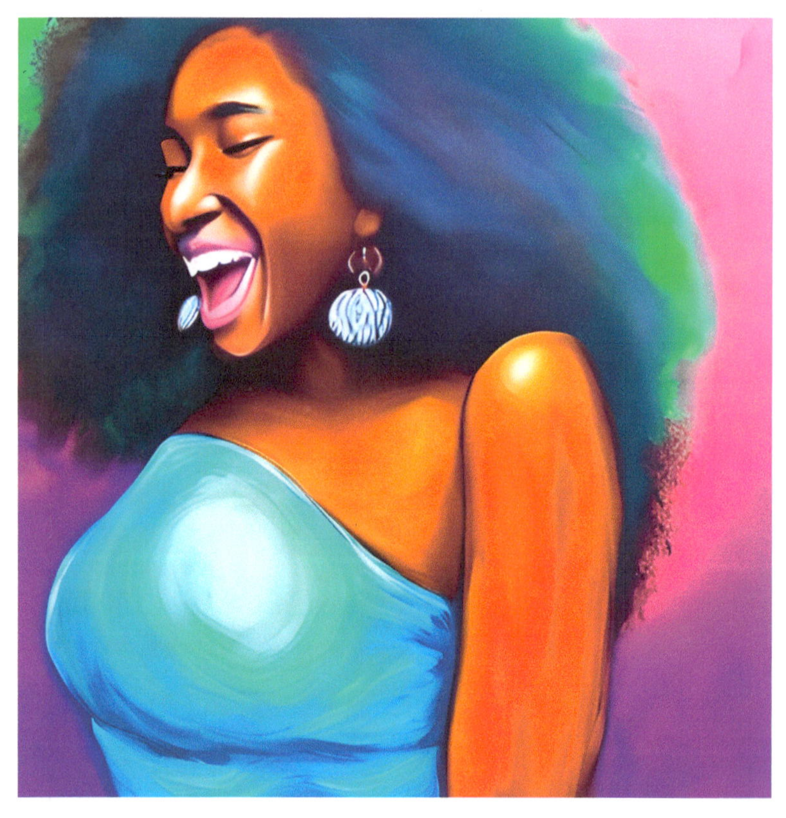

I deserve to be heard.

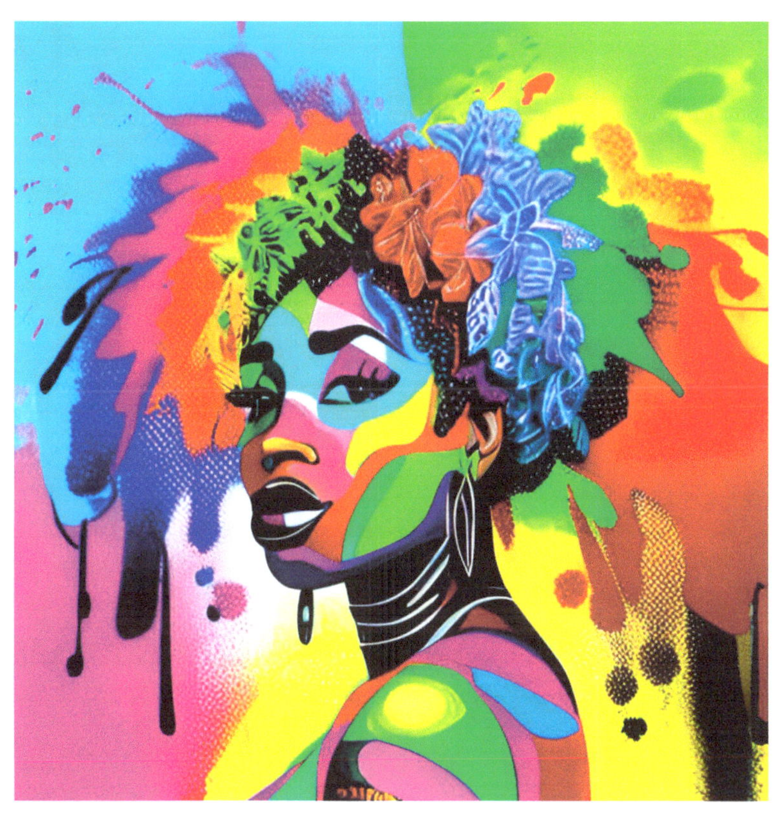

I am intelligent.

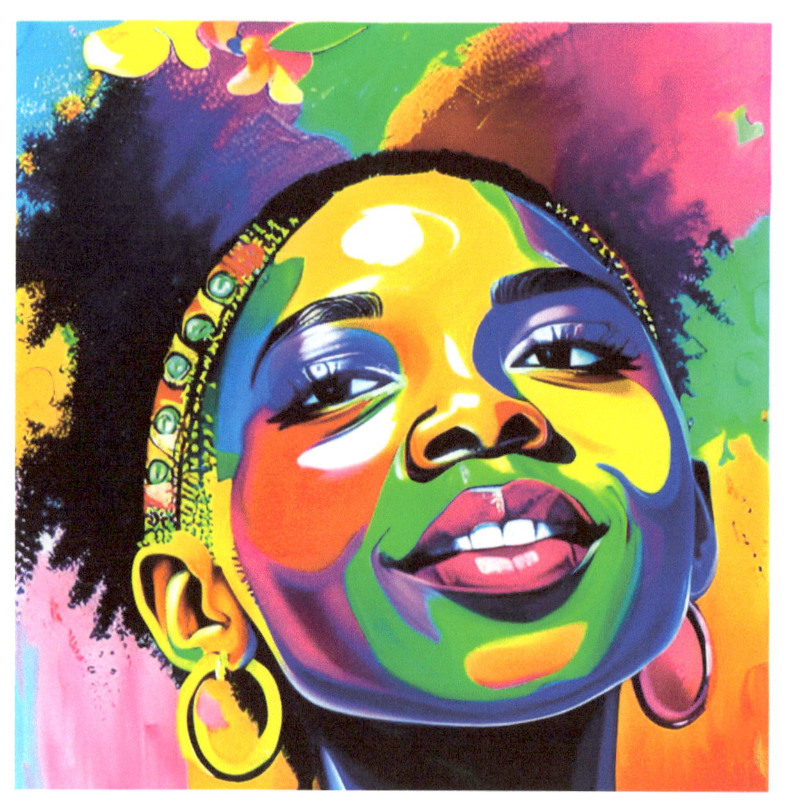

I think for myself.

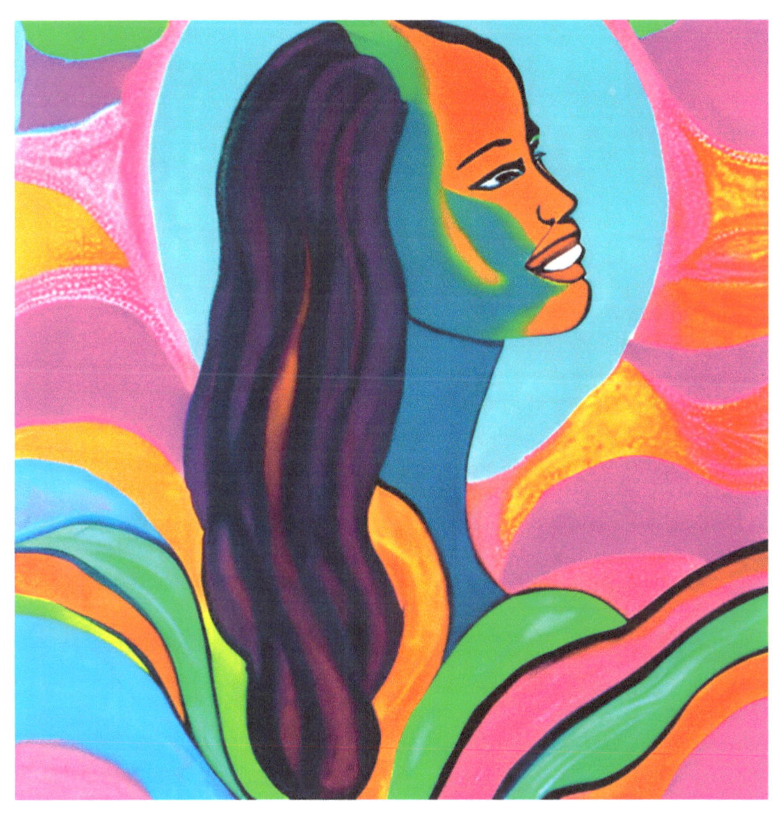

I am an inspiration to others.

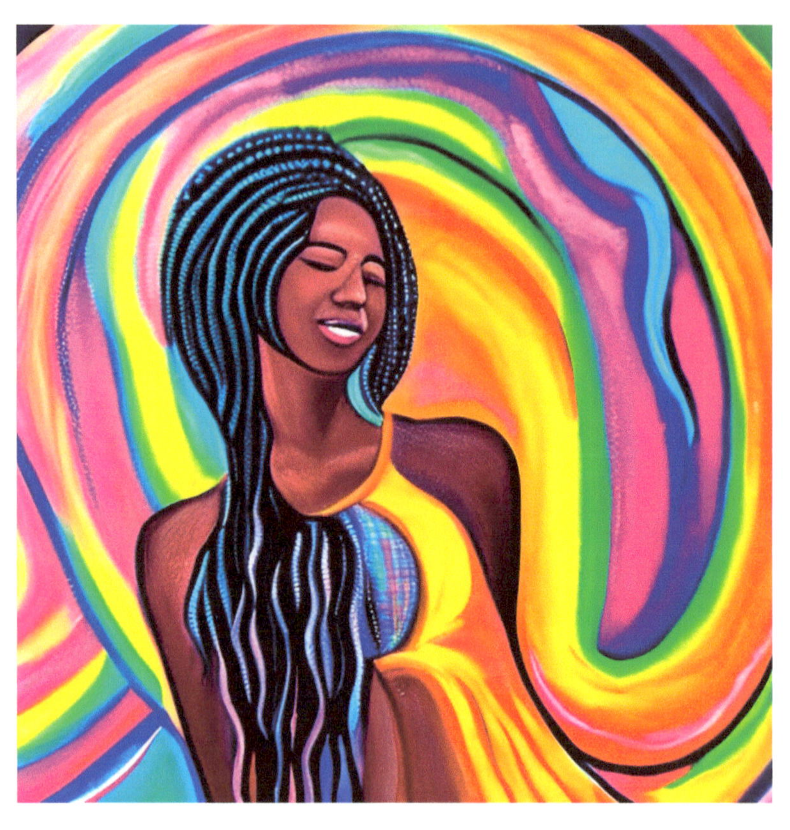

I speak my mind clearly.

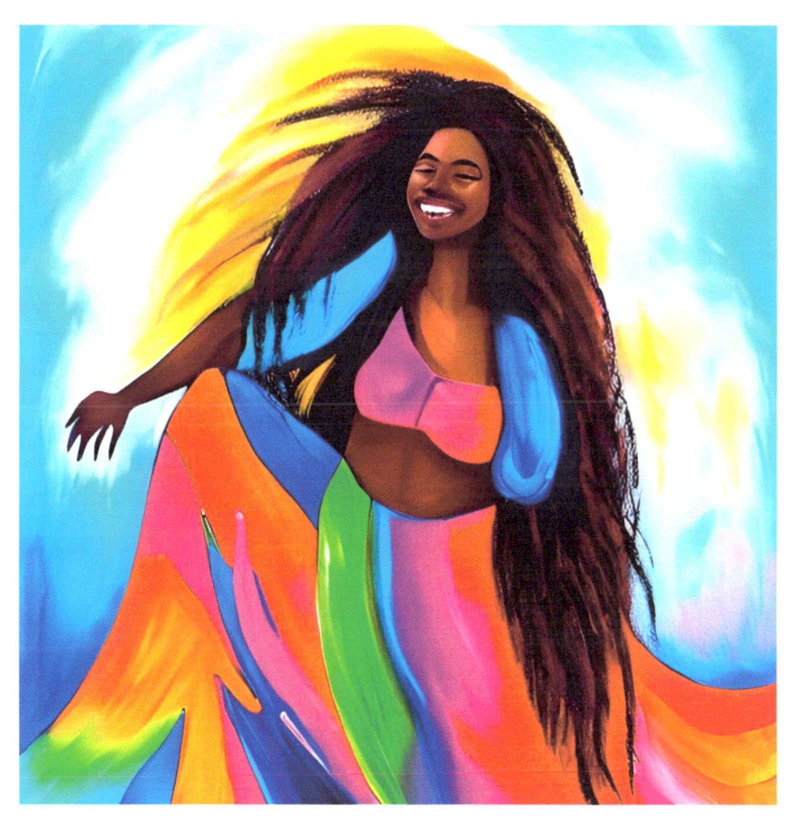

I attract positivity, love and light.

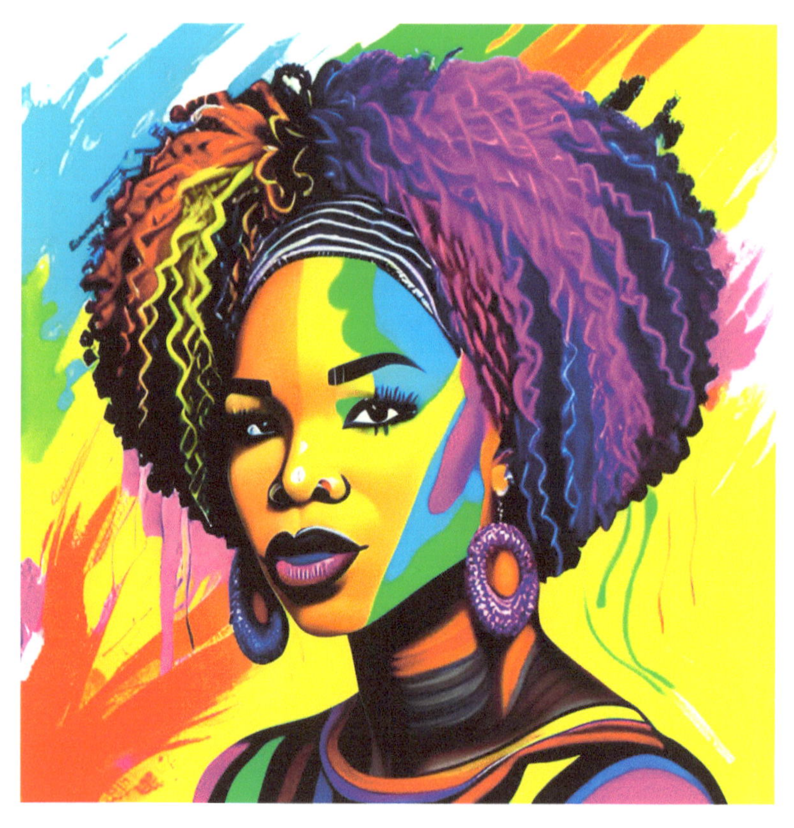

I am focused on my goals.

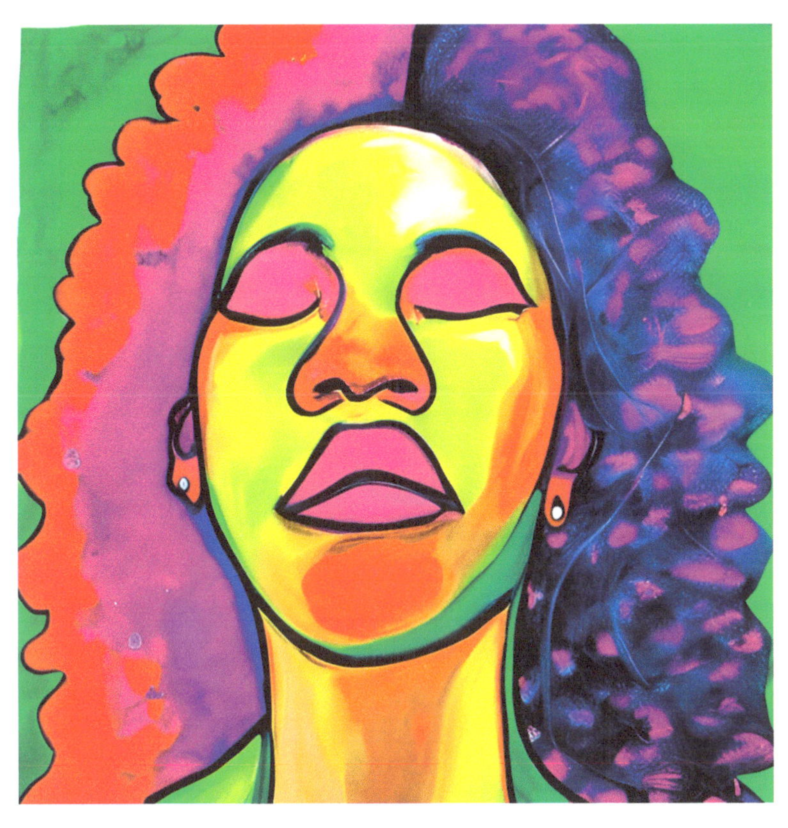

I breathe and release what's not meant for me.

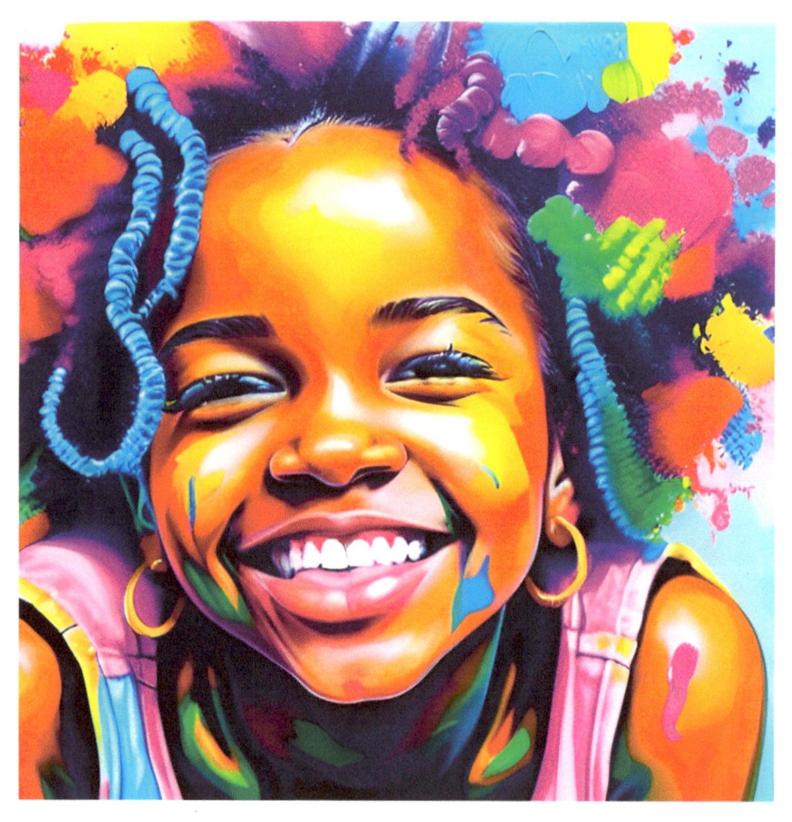

My skin glows like
magic.

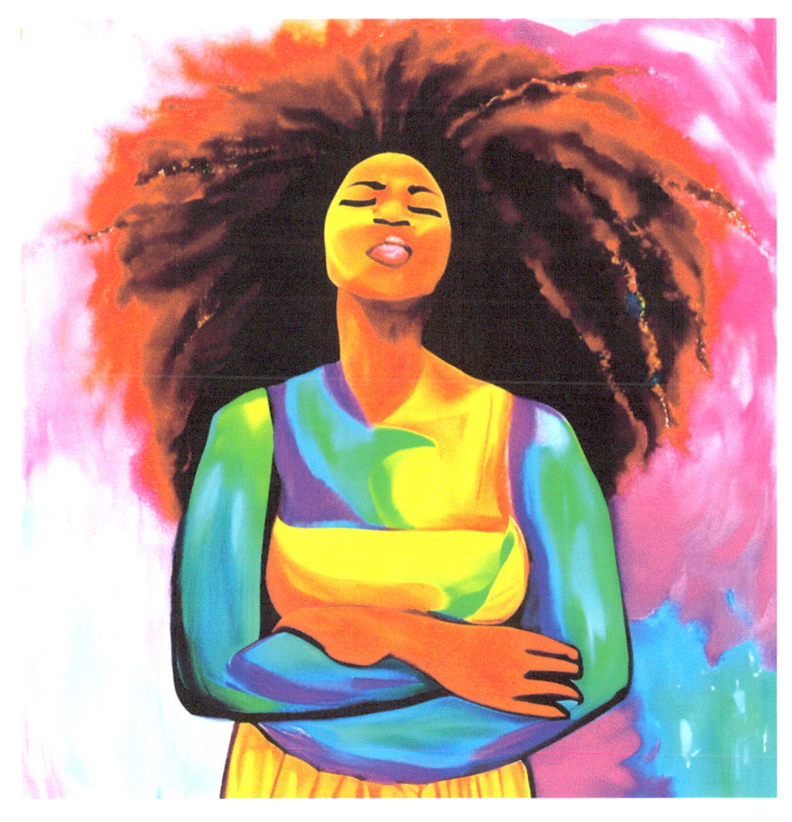

I am wild and free.

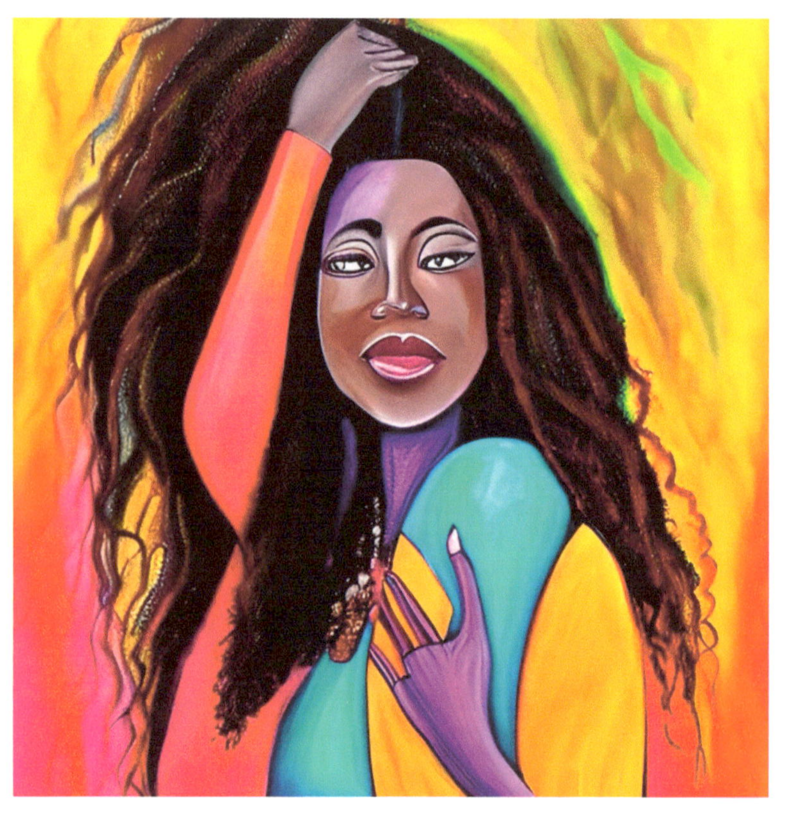

I am spiritual.

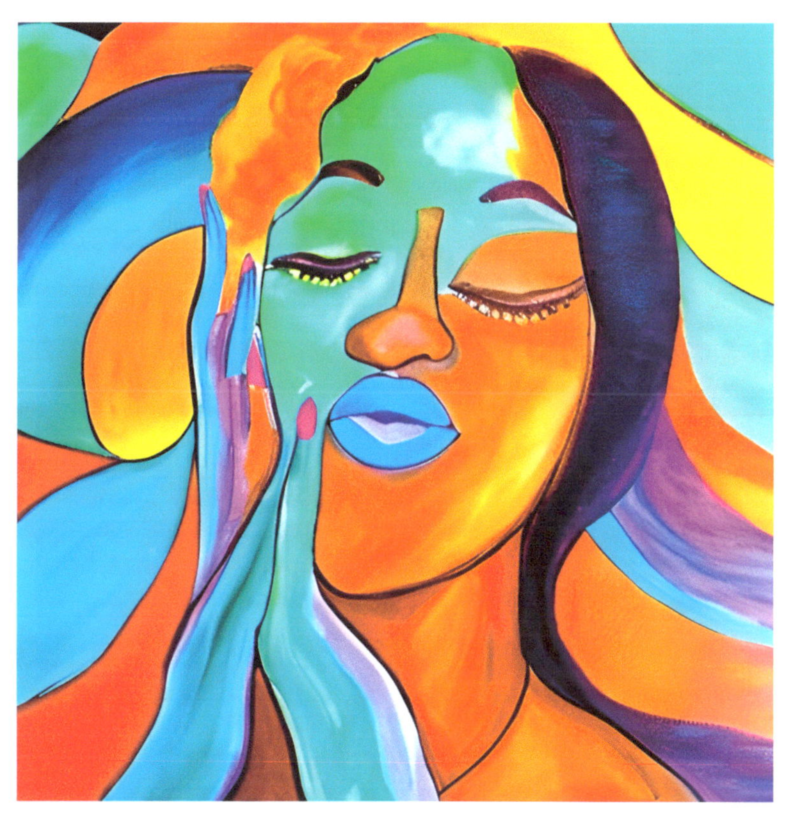

I am balanced and aligned.

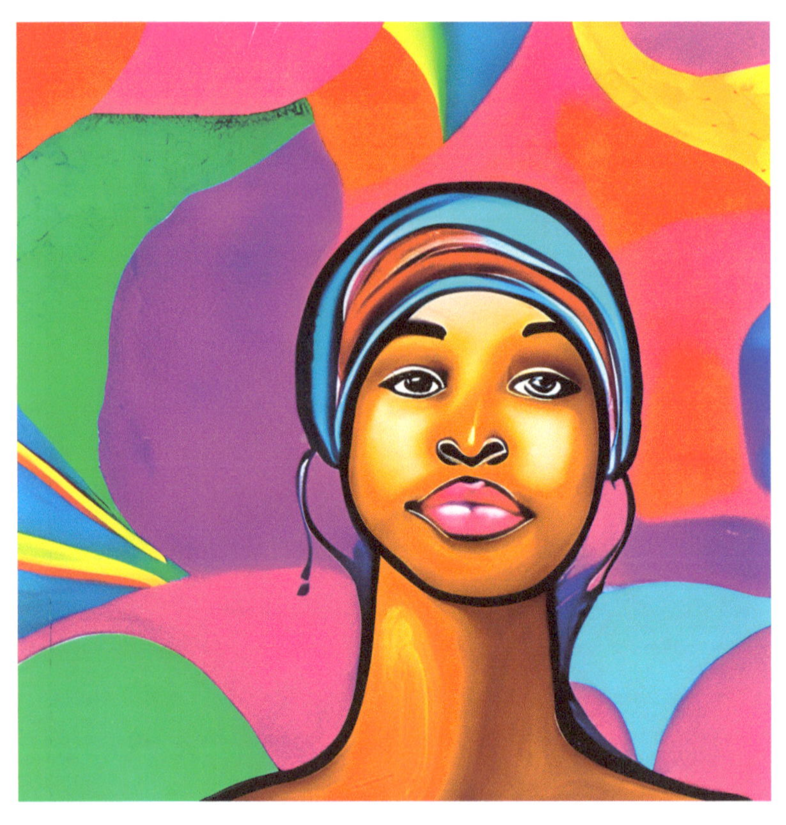

I am worthy of respect.

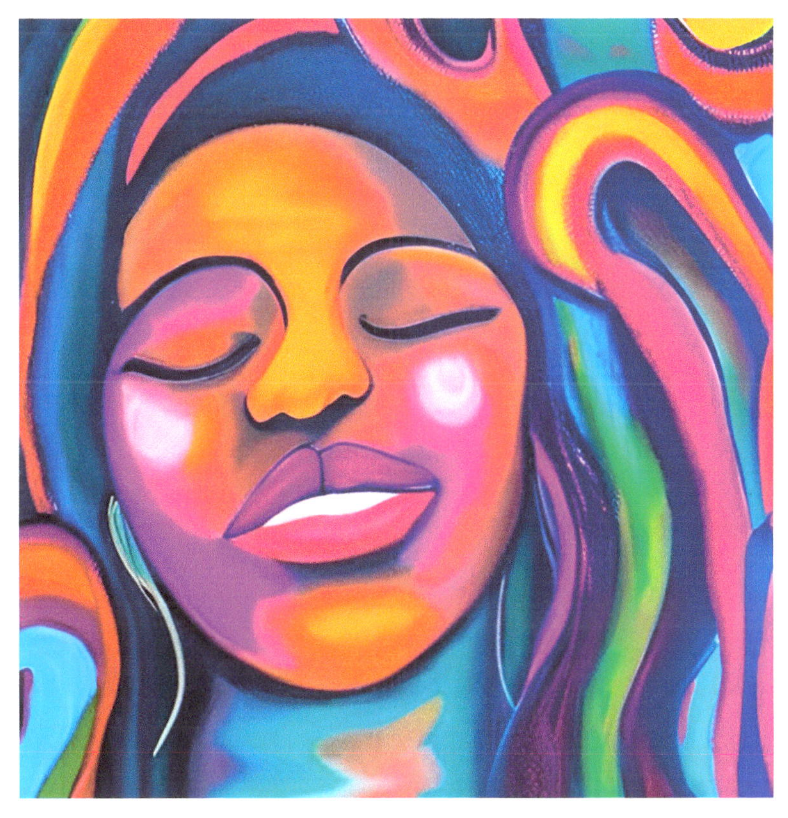

I am healthy in mind, body and spirit.

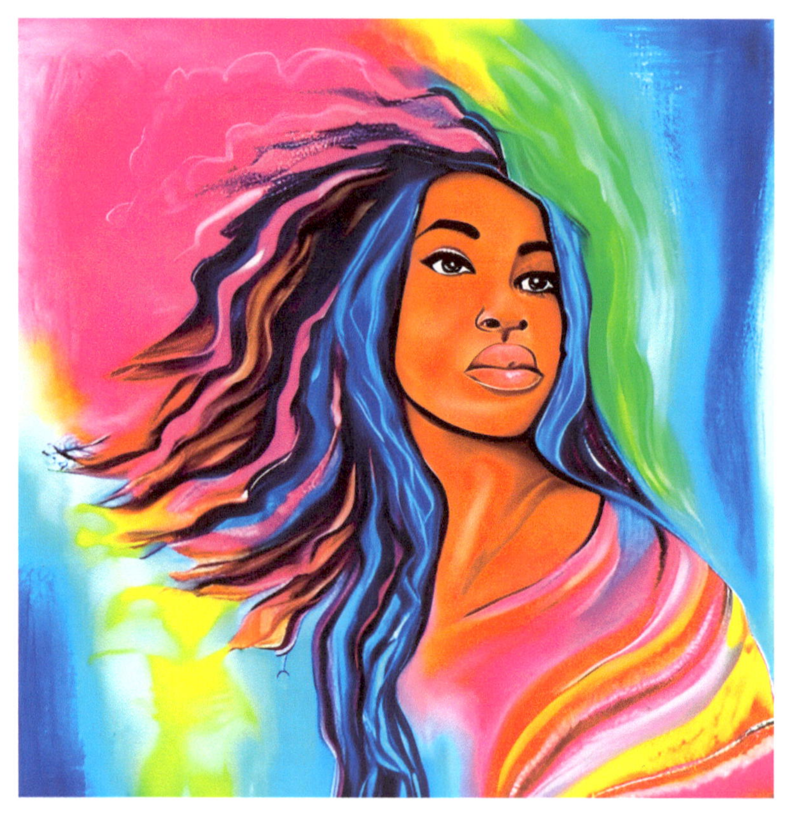

I am energy and manifestations.

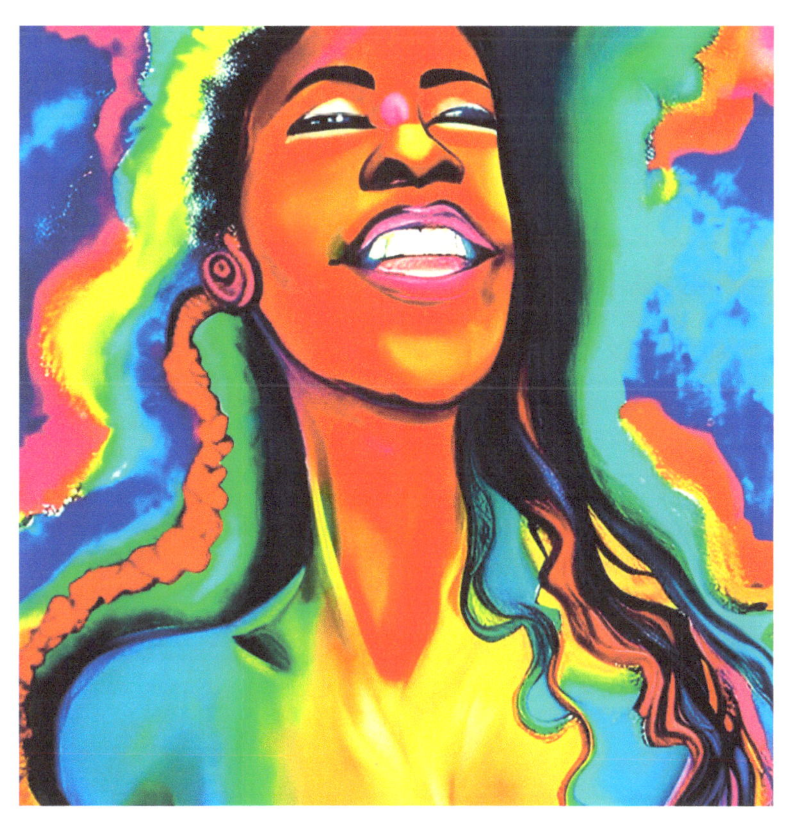

I am a teacher and a student.

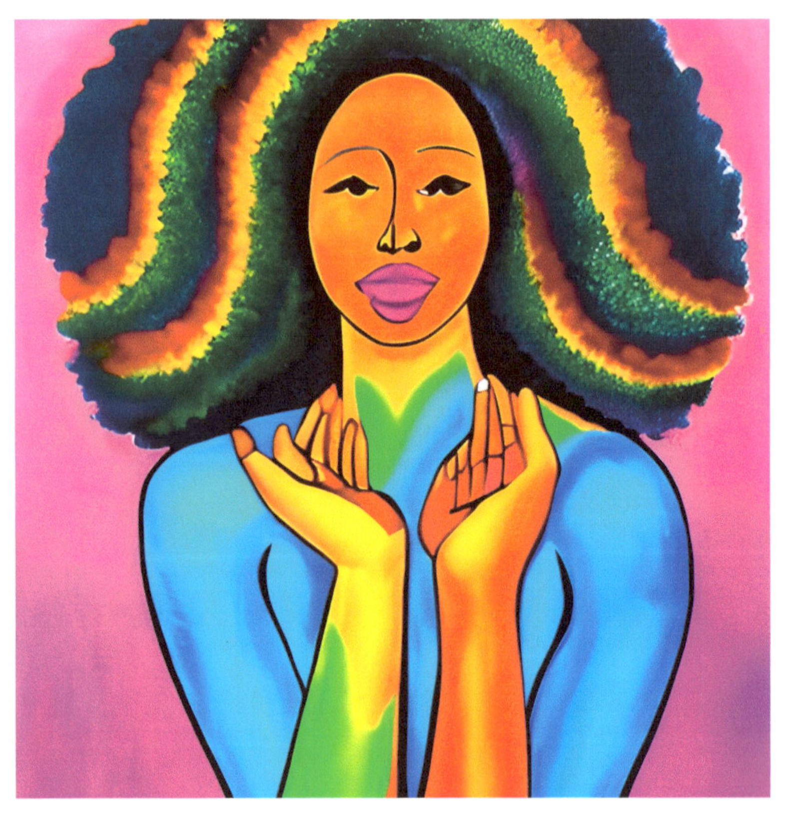

I respect myself and others.

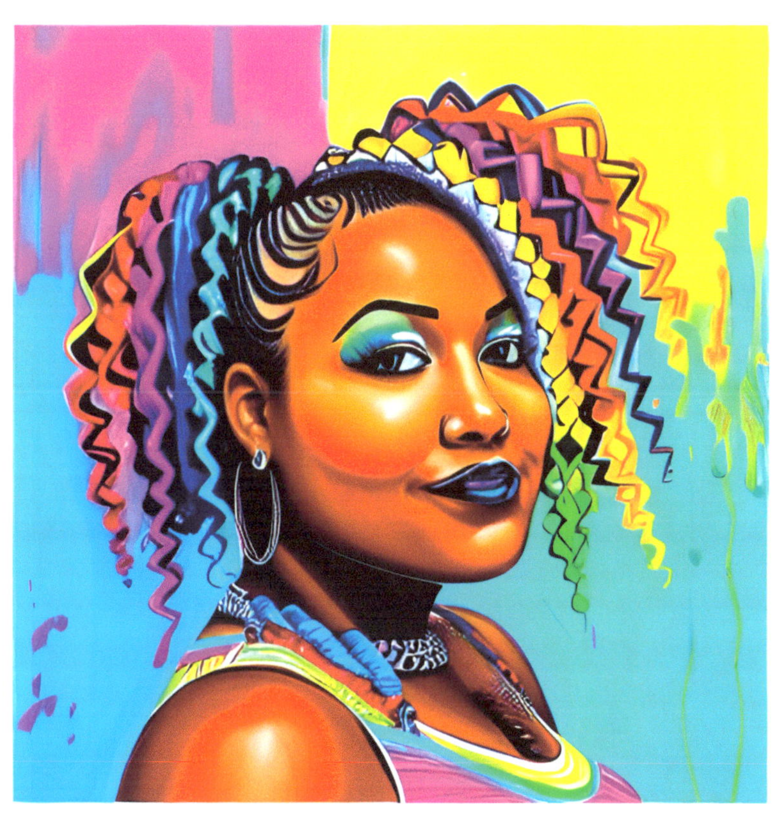

Empowering others empowers me.

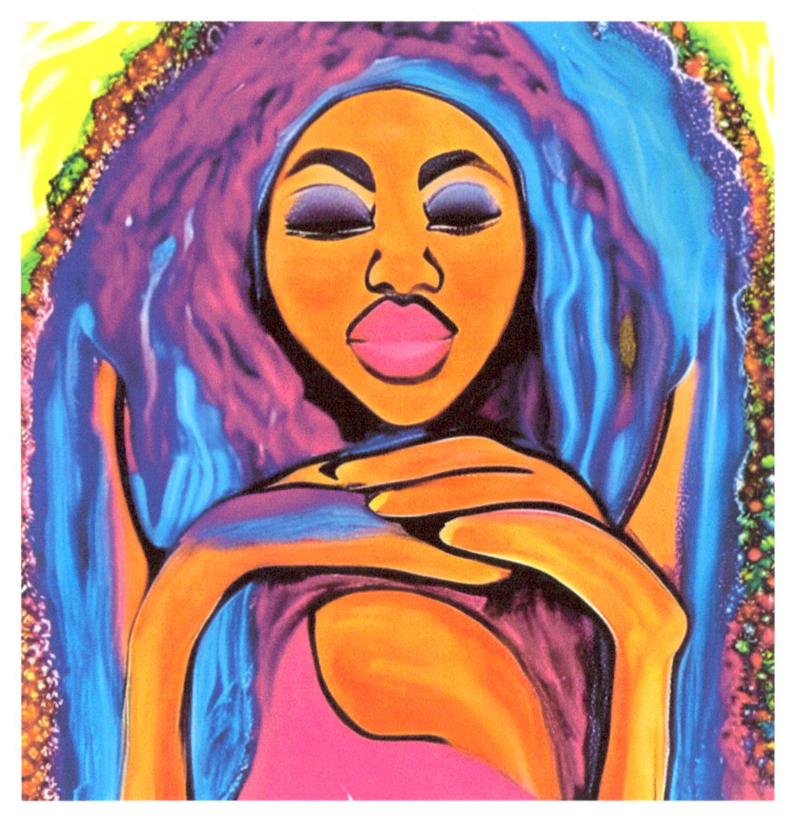

I am intelligence and gratitude.

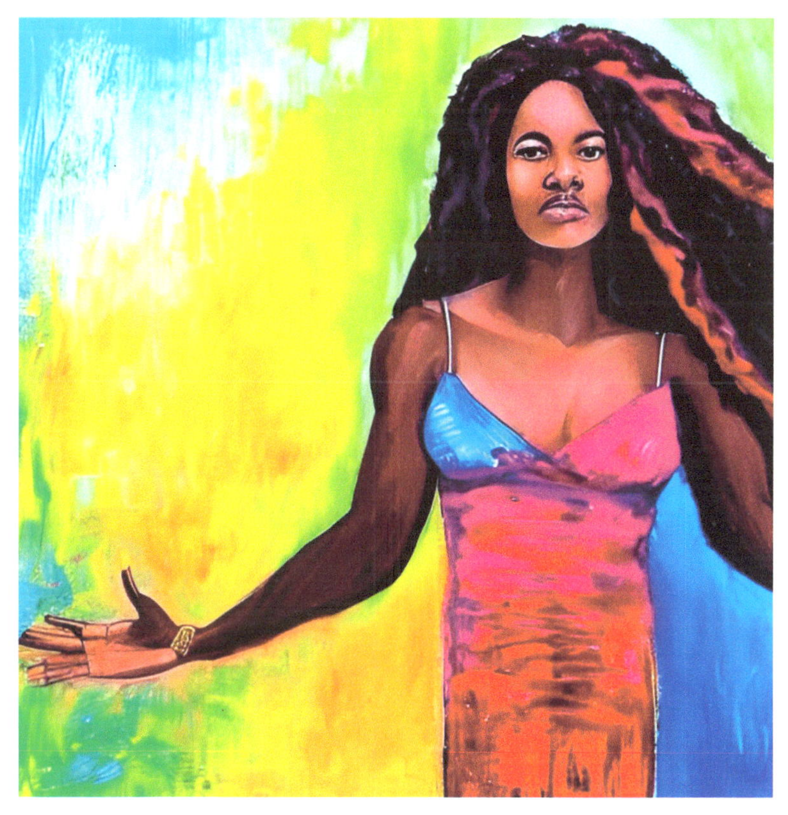

I am my ancestors.

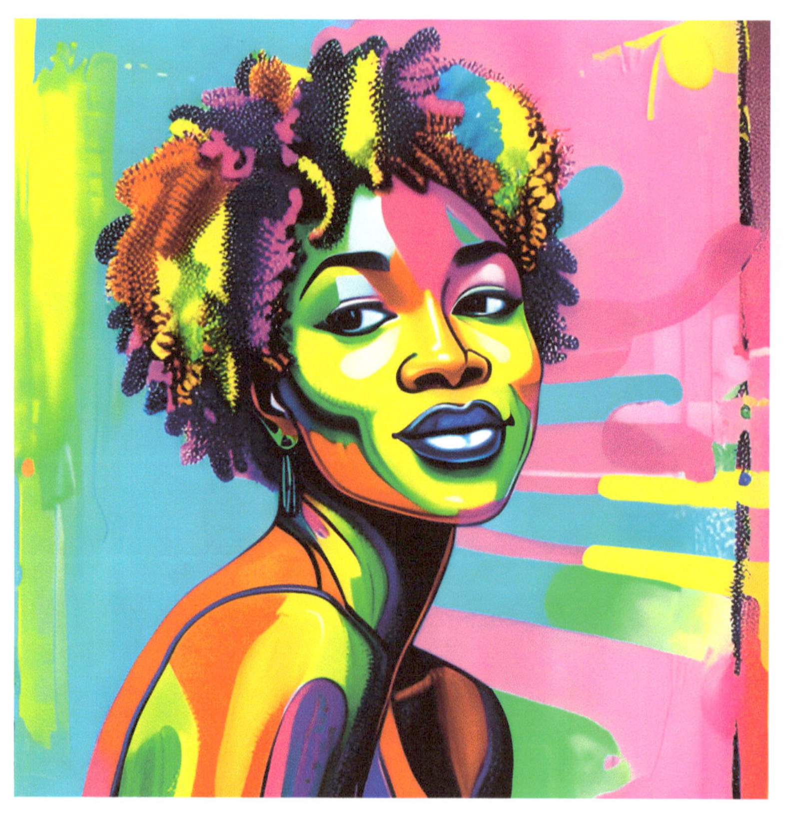

I am peaceful, honest and kind.

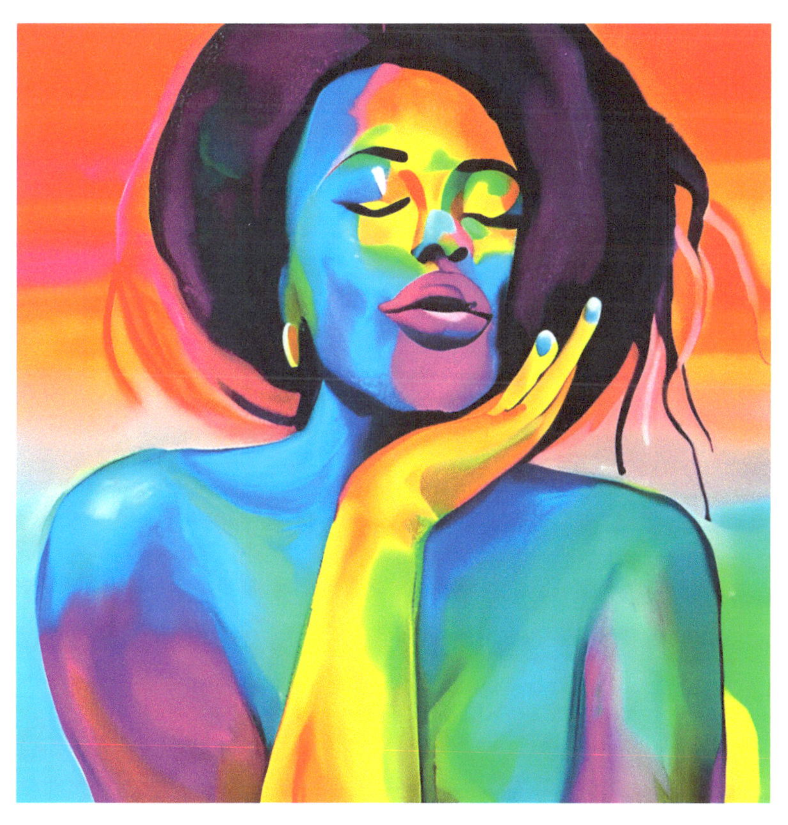

I am perfect the way I am.

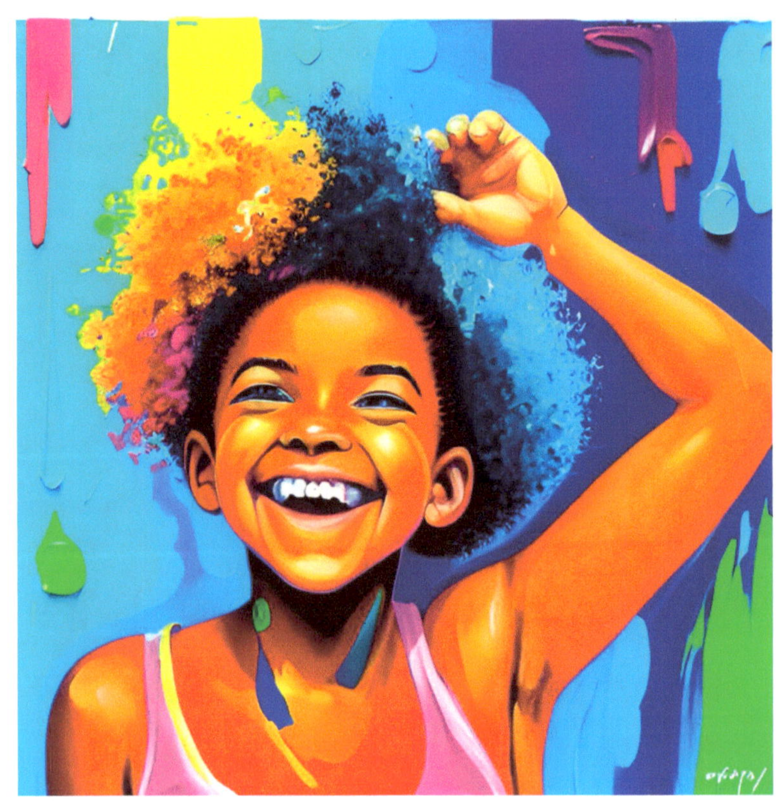

I am deserving of a healthy happy life.

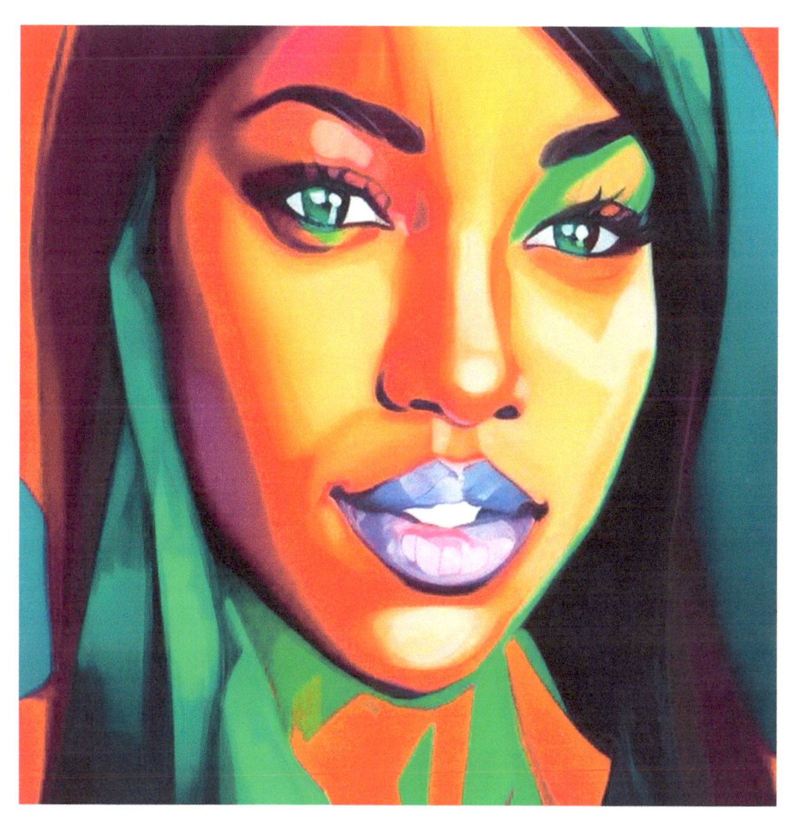

I am a story waiting to be heard.

I am black and proud.

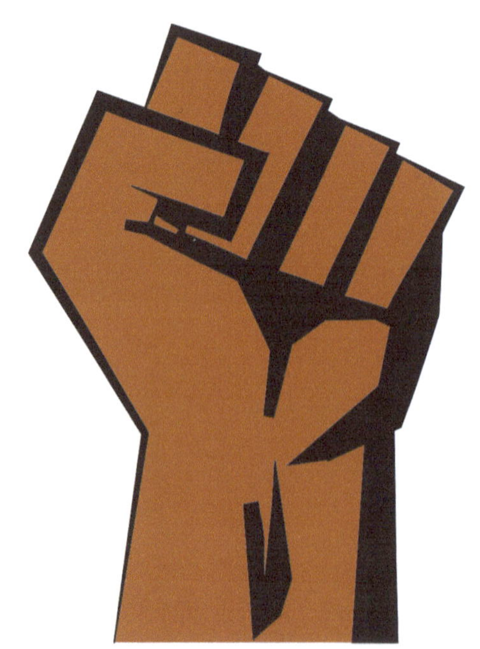

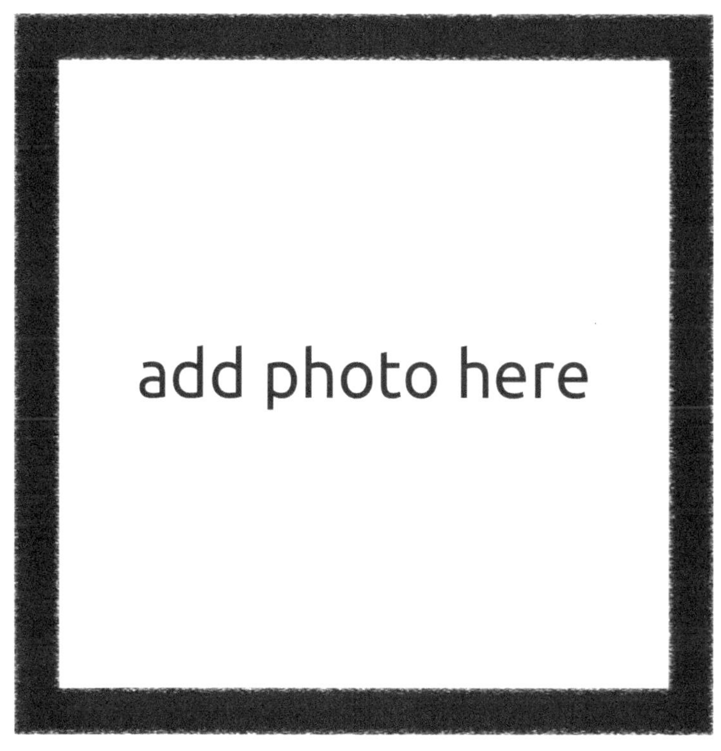

I am

name

www.ingramcontent.com/pod-product-compliance
Lightning Source LLC
LaVergne TN
LVHW052256100826
845147LV00001B/58
9781961005006